Praise

"Oh the joy, the freedom, when we finally receive healing from our deepest wounds! I'm so glad Ryan wrote this book!"
   –JOHN ELDREDGE, author and President of Wild at Heart

"It's not always the magnitude of life challenges, but how we relate to and deal with them that matters. Page by page, Ryan brings perspectives about trials, betrayal, and a diversity of life challenges in a way that seemingly dismantles the devastation that life difficulties can bring. He reveals with great clarity the value and strength that can be leveraged from hardships and shares ways to connect with God and others to minimize—even vaporize—the polarizing effects of adversity. Read it and reap!"
   –DEAN DEL SESTO, entrepreneur and four-time published author

"I have had a front-row seat, these last few years, to Miller's dedicated application of the ideas in this book to his own life. I have watched as God has continued to heal the wounds in his soul and his relationships and has caused him to flourish as a husband, father, and leader. Miller is not only a powerful leader and communicator. He is also a dedicated practitioner, willing to do the deep, hard work of soul sojourn. The results have been nothing short of remarkable. As a pastor, I have met with Miller and a group of men in our church every week for the past two years. During that time, I have seen God restore a highly gifted, yet wounded man, back to his calling to lead in the spheres of family, business, and church. I believe there is significant insight in this book that will help you greatly. More importantly, there is a life behind these ideas that is walking them out with integrity. And that is rare."
   –ALAN FROW, Lead Pastor of Southlands Church

WOUNDS

WOUNDS

HOW HURT, HEARTACHE, AND TRAGEDY BECOME THE KEYS TO UNLOCKING GREATNESS

RYAN JAMES MILLER

Copyright © 2023 Ryan James Miller

Wounds: How Hurt, Heartache, and Tragedy Become the Keys to Unlocking Greatness

All rights reserved.

First edition.

Hardcover ISBN: 979-8-9888514-2-4
Paperback ISBN: 979-8-9888514-3-1
Ebook ISBN: 979-8-9888514-1-7
Audiobook ISBN: 979-8-9888514-0-0

*This book is dedicated to the 6-year-old me.
I want you to know that it's going to be ok.*

*You are going to make a lot of big mistakes,
but it's going to be ok.
You are going to see some terrible things,
but it's going to be ok.
You are going to fall short and fail,
but it's going to be ok.*

*It's going to be ok because God will be with you.
It's going to be ok because God will provide for you.
It's going to be ok because God will reveal
the greatness He has in store for you.*

Contents

Foreword ix

Introduction xiii

Chapter 1: Wounded by Violence and Death 1

Chapter 2: Wounded by Abandonment 19

Chapter 3: Wounded by Lies and Loss 35

Chapter 4: Wounded by Selfishness and Sex 53

Chapter 5: Wounded by Brokenness 74

Chapter 6: Wounded by Failure 92

Chapter 7: Wounded by Unforgiveness 107

Chapter 8: Wounded by Unfair Accusations 120

Chapter 9: Wounded by Church 132

Conclusion 149

Acknowledgments 155

Foreword

OUR WOUNDS HAVE THE POWER TO TRANSFORM US.

Our wounds have the power to help us reach new heights or sink to familiar depths.

It's likely that you picked up this book because you follow Ryan Miller on social media or you've heard him speak recently and you're curious. Or, you've found yourself on the other side of a happy season and the title resonated with your pain.

Whatever the reason, as a former client and current friend, I can assure you that the following pages will not make you feel better, but you will feel stronger. I can assure you that you won't be all better tomorrow, but you will start to understand the root of your pain. I can assure you that perfection will never be yours, but that's never been Ryan's goal to help people achieve their ideal selves. He is called to grab a hand, look deep into the hearts of others and forge a bond founded on resilience over pain, drive over despair, and abiding in Jesus over self-reliance.

Early on in my business-owning career, I believed I had to wear the entrepreneur identity and make others believe I was more successful than I was. Not so much from a material standpoint. I wasn't buying fauxlexes and posting content to create a persona. It was more that I wanted to convince people of my sophistication, my panache, my *je ne sais quoi*.

I wanted people to know that I was a confident award-winning writer from a prestigious writer's program; that I'd been accepted to an exclusive writers conference; that I was a record-setting copywriter who quickly mastered the craft and learned how to sell far and above the rest of the team; that I was an entrepreneur, starting my second agency before turning thirty; and that I was newly married and everything there was as rock-solid as my faith in an all-loving, all-powerful God.

But, instead of actually doing those things, I was putting my energy into suppressing the facts: I wasn't writing, because I had a fear of success/failure. I had long bouts of imposter syndrome. Within a year of being a copywriter, I was so depressed that I actually contemplated suicide. The first agency I started was a failure because my business partner didn't like working with me. My amazing wife was unaware that I'd been struggling with pornography since middle school. And, most of all, I didn't believe in the love Jesus has for me that He'd professed throughout scripture.

I'm not sure we can isolate the source of every single wound. I'm not sure that's the point. What I know to be essential to not only making it to the next day, but also to actually being happy to wake up, is awareness. Awareness of the pain, the sorrow, the wounds that have scabbed over but still fester deep within. So deep I'd convinced myself it was better to fantasize about the already successful me than to, over time, learn to heal.

Ryan Miller entered my life in the midst of a tumultuous season. I was exactly a year into the next iteration of my business, on the therapy journey, and trying to simply get better by willing it into action. It was late 2012 in Fullerton, California, at a weekly networking breakfast I attended called Business Network International. Ryan sat down next to me, and I don't remember what we talked about other than that he was a sales coach and he too grew up in Yorba Linda.

I do remember that I had an interest in growing my sales and, thankfully, Ryan had an interest in securing more clients. We met, and I laid out my grand vision: *Get to the next day*. He listened and asked questions. We met again. And again. I won't bore you with the ins and outs of a client-advisor relationship. Ryan was instrumental in helping me break down barriers and achieve greater success. He pushed me, and I responded. What I did not expect was to meet someone, hire them to help me, and have them become one of my closest friends.

So what? Right?

Well, during that process of helping me understand my blockages and learn how to overcome them, Ryan was navigating rough waters. As you will read, he endured some of the most difficult challenges of his life. The advances I made in my life were in the midst of his tragedies. And therein lies one of the great aspects of this book: Our ability to help others grow and improve is not predicated on the idea that we've "made it" or achieved some level of success. It's our brokenness, our woundedness, that unleashes the power from God within to heal the whole body—the body of Christ, the believers.

Ryan is not perfect and never will be in this life. But that doesn't stop him from helping others reach new heights. By identifying the areas in which breakthroughs are hindered, and using Ryan's wounds as examples in the process, you will likely discover new layers that need time to be understood and processed. That's OK. One of the great fallacies of this world is that we can heal quickly, that being wounded is a weakness.

Instead of trying to get better right away, go into this book with a readiness to uncover areas of pain and hurt. Know that by uncovering them, you start the healing process. Trust that you're on the journey with someone who's unashamed of their scars.

—John Welches
Yorba Linda, California
May 2023

Introduction

IN APRIL 2019, I EXPERIENCED WHAT WAS DIAGNOSED AS MY FIRST anxiety attack.

Sure, I'd felt anxious before. I'd had dark and lowly days. But something about that day was different. The weeks leading up to that moment weren't the best. I'd lost out on a pretty significant business opportunity that would have paid me very well over the course of the year, and I was walking through a very difficult situation with a friend regarding his marriage. Those two challenges were capped off by my most significant stressor: my business. I owned a consulting and coaching practice, and was helping a client redevelop their sales process while also coaching four of their salespeople to exceed revenue goals. This particular client was my largest, with a monthly five-figure contract. And I was on the verge of losing them.

When I woke up that day, knowing I would receive a call from my client later in the morning, I went dark. Doubt set in about my true calling, my capabilities, and even my self-worth. I tried to fight through it. I imagined retired Navy SEAL and ultramarathon runner David Goggins telling me to stop being such a little bitch, but it didn't work. It was difficult to drive the three miles to my office, but I had work to do, clients to help.

I got through one coaching call...barely. But as I got closer to talking to my client, to losing that contract, my thoughts spiraled. *How will my family pay our bills? How quickly will we be right back to 2013, when we lost everything? What will I tell my family? What might other people think? I cannot stomach another failure like this.*

I sat in the corner of my office and curled into a ball. My body was shutting down. Physically, I felt the energy was being sucked out of me. Mentally, I had a hard time engaging the logic of what was happening. And spiritually, I cried out to God in what felt like faint whispers. I had one last option in the moment. I called my wife and begged her to pray for me. I told her what was happening and how I was feeling. She prayed on the phone with me, and she continued to pray for me throughout the day.

By God's grace, I made it through that day. My wife's prayers, along with God's Spirit, brought comfort to my soul. It also helped that when I got the call from my client later that day, it was only to discuss reconfiguring the execution of our work, not to adjust the fees or cancel the contract.

In the days and weeks to follow, through lots of prayer and discussion with others close to me, I analyzed what happened to me that day. Was my anxiety attack simply the culmination of too much bad news in a short period of time, or was there something deeper?

Because circumstances can trigger events like the one I experienced, I realized my anxiety attack was the result of a wound... well, many wounds actually. You see, my stress over the potential loss of the client wasn't the worst thing that had ever happened to me—far from it. The potential loss was simply the emotional hit that opened up a host of old wounds. The wounds I speak of are not outward, physical cuts, scrapes, or bruises to the body. They are long-held emotional injuries that, when left untreated, fester and worsen over time.

Every human being on this earth has been wounded. You picked up this book because you understand that. Wounds deep down inside of you have been bandaged over in hopes that they would just heal on their own. But bandages do nothing for deep wounds created the moment a parent walked out of your life or when a loved one was tragically killed without notice. The self-inflicted wounds from drug and alcohol addiction don't go away just because you wish

INTRODUCTION

they would. And the wounds that come from familiar people and places, like church, seem particularly difficult to forget no matter how hard we try.

One might think we would be expertly equipped to deal with wounds, considering the brokenness of this world and the constant afflictions we face. From the time I was young, like many boys, I incurred visible wounds, like deep cuts and broken bones from playing sports and crashing my dirt bike. I was often told to get up, shake it off, tape 'em up, and keep going. This is the norm, especially for boys, isn't it? So, it's no wonder that when the wounds are mental and emotional, as we grow up, we attempt to use the same prescription. I was conditioned to believe I could just dust off the hurt from my parents' divorce, bury the loss when my business nearly failed shortly after its launch, and bulldoze through the death and destruction I witnessed during the Las Vegas mass shooting.

"I can do all things through Him who strengthens me" becomes the war cry for most Christians who attempt to try harder and push through trauma. But that doesn't work in the same way as resetting a broken bone. Worse, most emotional wounds are more severe than a broken bone. They are more like a compound fracture of the femur that has blown right through the thigh. And our answer to that mess is to clothe our inner turmoil in a T-shirt with Philippians 4:13 written on it. But we keep bleeding right through that shirt, continuing to writhe in pain.

Many look to anything that might take the pain away, turning to self-preservation or self-medication. Some might read another book on grittiness, watch a motivational talk about mindset, or drink until the pain numbs. None of those tactics works in the long term. The wound is left untreated, and every attempt to make the wound disappear becomes a potential contributor to one's absolute destruction.

In my case, as I got older, my wounds got bigger. And the bigger my wounds got, the harder it was to shake them off. I couldn't make them go away. Past wounds came back to haunt me, leading to more wounds, which were often self-inflicted. My wounds smoldered as I became more stressed, anxious, frustrated, and angry, and I didn't know what to do about it. By the time I was twenty-eight years old, I felt lost. Though everyone saw a successful man building a life for himself and his family, I was a broken, hollow shell of a human being.

Thankfully, that brokenness led me to discover a relationship with God. That relationship did not immediately heal my wounds. In fact, I'd incur some of my deepest wounds after becoming a Christian. Instead, my relationship with God helped to reveal my wounds and give me a process to heal from them.

Though I had been a Christian for thirteen years, my anxiety attack in 2019 was the result of defaulting back to self-medication and self-preservation. Before knowing Christ, I used social norms like alcohol, drugs, gambling, and male bravado to mask all of my pain. Leading up to my anxiety attack, I had turned to working harder, ignoring the fact that I couldn't outwork or outrun what was hurting inside. Every one of those tactics only worsened the situations, the wounds, and my overall well-being.

After my anxiety attack, reflecting back on my first encounter with Jesus reminded me that I bore my wounds for a reason—two reasons actually. The first was to coax me back into the arms of Jesus, who was always there to comfort and strengthen me. God was reminding me over and over again that I couldn't flourish on my own—I needed Him. The second reason was so God could further open my mind, to show me I could go beyond simply owning my wounds. I learned to address them, grow from them, relate to others through them, and, ultimately, leverage them to discover and hone God's calling on my life so I could achieve the greatness for which He created me.

This process became what I call the Wound-Analysis Framework, a series of three steps designed to help me deal with my spiritual and emotional wounds:

1. **Acknowledge the hurt.** The first step is to identify painful experiences that wounded me.

2. **Realize the effect.** Next, I accept the emotional impact those experiences have had on me.

3. **Unlock the greatness.** Finally, I dig into those emotions to mine for lessons I can glean to strengthen myself spiritually, emotionally, mentally, and physically.

As I share in this book some of my life's darkest moments, I demonstrate the Wound-Analysis Framework as the tool God gave me to unlock greatness from inside each and every wound I bore.

In a decades-long journey to get where I am, I have learned so much and grown immensely.

As a performance coach, I have worked with hundreds of executives and entrepreneurs. This has allowed me to study human behavior, psychology, and how an individual's wounds often hold them back from the success they dream of.

As a pastor, I've walked through life with numerous individuals, couples, and families, observing how they experienced and dealt with wounds, as well as establishing how I could best support them during those seasons and ultimately point them to Jesus.

As a man who had to grow up too quickly, was often influenced to make poor choices, and tried every way he could think of to create a great life on his own, I left a trail of wounds that hurt those I loved and cared about the most—myself included.

My hope is that by reading this book, you will feel led to take the following actions:

First, permit yourself to tap into and share your wounds. Being vulnerable about the events that have hurt you the deepest is not a weakness but rather a strength. Leaning into that strength makes you even stronger.

Second, break out of the prison in which you are living. Emotional prison for most people looks like this: You're bound by shame tied to the ways you have hurt yourself or how others have hurt you. To feel good about yourself, you constantly seek validation from others. You struggle to maintain a good balance of physical, mental, emotional, and spiritual health. You want to make God a priority, but you just can't seem to do that consistently.

Third, discover your purpose. The process of self-discovery was incredibly fruitful for me, but it wasn't voluntary and often came on the other side of great physical, emotional, mental, and spiritual pain. My hope is that as you acknowledge the hurt, realize its effect, and unlock your greatness, you will enable yourself to live the life for which God created you.

It's time to unlock the greatness that's already inside of you!

1

WOUNDED BY VIOLENCE AND DEATH

WHAT IN THE HELL AM I DOING WITH MY LIFE?

Eighteen months prior to my first anxiety attack, I sat in a different office, in a different professional role, and asked myself that question. For what felt like the tenth time in my life, I was deeply hurting and in crisis, struggling to understand what to do with what I was experiencing.

As I walked into The Centennial Group office in mid-October 2017, my coworkers did their best to welcome me back to work without overwhelming me. After many hugs and a few tears, I made my way to my corner office. I closed the door behind me and took a deep breath as I sat down in my chair. I turned on my computer, and it started to boot up, making the same sound it had thousands of times before. I thought, *Will doing the things I've always done help me get back to normal? What is normal?*

I spun around in my chair and looked out the floor-to-ceiling window toward the Newport coast. I don't know what I was looking for, or hoping for—possibly soaking in the beauty of creation in an attempt to ward off my horrific thoughts of the past two weeks. I feared the sounds of automatic gunfire and people screaming. I was sickened by visions of bloodstained walls, injured victims, and even dead bodies.

Then it hit me, seemingly out of nowhere: *What in the hell are you doing with your life?*

For most people in my position, that would have seemed a crazy question. I was more in love with my wife than ever, and our marriage was extremely healthy. My two daughters were doing very well, and our immediate family of four loved spending as much time together as we could. At thirty-nine years old, I was in the best physical shape of my life. And I was working for a pretty good company, making a healthy six-figure annual salary with great benefits and a stock package.

But the reason behind that question came from one of the deepest wounds I have ever endured—being present for the mass shooting at the Route 91 Harvest music festival in Las Vegas, Nevada, on October 1, 2017.

A THREE-DAY NEON SLEEPOVER

The year prior, our friends—Chad, Nicol, and Tracy—convinced me and my wife, Michelle, to join them for Route 91 Harvest, an annual three-day country music festival on the Vegas strip.

Chad, Nicol, and Tracy were what Michelle and I called our "framily"—a close group of a dozen friends who grew up together, shared monumental life moments, and treated one another like family. Chad and I have known each other since shortly after birth, growing up on the same street. We rode bikes and played basketball in our hometown of Yorba Linda, California. We toilet-papered houses and even broke a few laws. Chad's transition back into "normal life" after a few years of playing professional baseball with the New York Mets had him basically living with me and Michelle. Chad is one of my best friends—someone I love with all my heart. He has always, and will always, have my back.

In many ways, Tracy and Nicol were a pair of peas in a pod, loud and boisterous, and always ready for a great time. Tracy and I grew up on the same street, but we grew closest during the three years leading up to Route 91 Harvest 2016. Nicol was newer to the group, but her magnetic and joyful personality made her an easy friend to love quickly. While Chad, Tracy, and Nicol were technically single, Chad and Nicol had a special relationship that looked to everyone like they were dating, even if the two were unwilling to admit it.

Michelle and I loved being with all of them.

Our first year together at Route 91 Harvest was incredible. During the daytime, the pool area provided space to enjoy a few cocktails and relax. Vegas can be fast-paced, so we took advantage of the time to slow down a little and recharge. Our nights were all about singing and dancing, with a few cocktails as we went along, in an environment that always felt welcoming, caring, and supportive. Country music people, including the concertgoers and the artists, are a unique group. They perceive one another as family, and the Route 91 Harvest crowd was the typical model for that community. I love country music because it puts so much emphasis on faith in God and love for our country—both critical to living an amazing and free life.

After that awesome weekend, Michelle and I were committed to going back to the festival every year thereafter. Waiting for the 2017 event was like being a kid waiting for Christmas day, every day, for damn near a year. The closer it got to the festival, the more excited we became. We chose themed outfits for each night of the concert, and we planned our breakfast spots, pool times, and daily arrivals at the concert venue.

By the time the 2017 artist lineup was announced, we were out of our minds fired up. Morgan Wallen and Luke Combs—this was before they were big stars—were performing on the Next from Nashville stage. The main stage was to include performances by Eric Church, Sam Hunt, Brothers Osborne, and Jason Aldean. Of them all, I was most excited for Jason Aldean. I'd never seen him in concert before, and I loved his music.

On Friday, September 29, 2017, Michelle and I packed up the car and headed out from Yorba Linda for the four-hour drive. Once in Las Vegas, our first stop was Mandalay Bay, our favorite Vegas hotel. We'd stayed there a dozen or so times over the years. The property was always well taken care of, the rooms were nice, and the pool was the bomb. We had our favorite bars and even knew of a very cool speakeasy inside the hotel.

We met up with quite a few people that first night, in addition to the 2016 crew of Chad, Tracy, and Nicol. Our core group grew when more of our framily, Casey and Heather, joined. We ran back and forth between stages, hit up vendors, and staked out our spot for the long run of big artists on opening night. Epic that night was an unforgettable performance by Brothers Osborne. I joined a symphony of 20,000 clapping hands to "It Ain't My Fault." We were one people, not to be divided by gender, race, or religion, celebrating the fact that together we were "guilty of a damn good time," as the song lyrics say. If I close my eyes right now, I still see the images. The second day was equally amazing, highlighted by Sam Hunt's beats finding their way to the depths of my soul.

But day three was where it was at. Normally, by the third day of any festival, most people are low on steam. Two full days of dancing and partying does a number on ya. But this year, there was too much anticipation for that to happen. The early artists were great, but Big & Rich took the whole crowd to another place, leading us in "God Bless America." It was their moment to rise up against all the division in our country, reminding us that the United States is the most amazing country in the world, a country we are beyond blessed to live in. We lit our lighters, turned on our cell phone flashlights, and lit up that Vegas sky. It was so emotional.

The crowd was ready for Jason Aldean to take the stage, hitting our final wind to sing and dance for as long as he would lead us. The crowd went nuts as Aldean opened his show, and during the length of five songs, we were as high as life could take us.

But halfway through "Any Ol' Barstool," something happened. At first, it sounded like fireworks in the distance. Listening back to the cell phone video I have of that moment, I can hear people cheering, "Fireworks!"

Little did we know those were the test shots of a monster ready to unleash his hell on us.

WHEN HELL CAME TO EARTH

My framily and I were posted on the front right side of the stage, the area of the venue closest to the Mandalay. The first round of concentrated gunfire hit the ground approximately fifty feet from us, appearing as if someone had dropped a brick of firecrackers on the ground. But it was unsettling—we had never seen firecrackers set off at a country show.

As the second round of fire riddled the scene, the situation got real. Within seconds, Jason Aldean and his band sprinted off the stage, and all the lights in the venue went dark. The crowd panicked, but nobody knew exactly what to do, so we froze. I looked around to see where the firing was coming from, also trying to gauge the crowd's reaction. I saw, on moonlit faces across the crowd, confusion and fear—a combination I knew could easily lead to erratic and dangerous behavior.

As the third round of gunfire erupted, we all hit the ground. Michelle's screams cut through the crowd noise. She was right next to me, but my back was to her. My adrenaline spiked, and a brief sickness hit my stomach. The worst came to mind. *Is she hurt? Is she hit? If she's been hit, what should I do? God, please, I pray she wasn't hit.*

Thankfully, she was hurt only because someone else went down on top of her, crushing her leg. I pushed them off, grabbed Michelle, and started to pop back up. It was a welcome moment of relief but lasted only a second or two, because just then, Michelle said, "I think Nicol is hit!"

Nicol was face down, with what looked to be a bullet entry through the lower right side of her back. As Chad turned her over, blood came through her shirt. Chad put his finger directly into the bullet hole to try and stop her bleeding, but it wasn't working. The scene was so chaotic, bullets still flying around us, people screaming and dealing with their own devastation. Yet Nicol was so calm—no screaming, no crying, just a faint voice saying, "My legs are going numb."

"What do we do?" I asked.

Chad replied, "We need to try and get her up, and move her somewhere safer."

Tracy held her hand, repeatedly telling her, "It's OK, baby girl."

We weren't sure, but it seemed as though the gunfire was coming from street level over the wall. That created a greater sense of urgency for me and Chad to get Nicol—and all of us—to safety. The fourth round of gunfire rained down, and everyone went again to the ground. I jumped on top of Michelle to shield her body, clinching tighter than I ever had. My eyes were closed, and I knew I could take a bullet at any moment. I was so scared, but the choice was clear. If someone had to die, it wouldn't be Michelle.

When the shots stopped, Chad and I attempted to move Nicol. He got under her shoulders, and I got her legs. She was limp, which made it hard to gain leverage to pick her up. Adding to the difficulty was the fact that I wouldn't take my eyes off Michelle and made sure she held onto me the entire time.

That break in gunfire was the green light for people to scramble. We assumed gunfire would resume momentarily, and nobody wanted to be a sitting duck. I've never served in the military or been to war, but instinct kicked in. I needed to protect my wife, the mother of my children, at all costs.

I grabbed Michelle to make sure she didn't get trampled. Chad and I tried one more time, but we couldn't lift Nicol. "We can't move her!" I yelled. Chad acknowledged with a nod. His face showed that he felt defeated, deflated.

The gunfire, relentless, at times flew right past us. We had to get out of there. I'd made a choice to protect Michelle *at all costs*, and I knew that meant leaving behind any chance to help pull Nicol out.

Michelle and I ran about one hundred feet toward a small row of bleachers. My intention was to get under the bleachers with Michelle, to shield us from gunfire. By the time we got there, it was packed like sardines. There was no more room underneath, so we sheltered in place in front of them. We were partially protected by railings, but no solid divider stood between us and the shots. It was frightening to know we weren't fully protected, but it was the best we could do.

Gunshots ricocheted off of the metal. People under the bleachers screamed and cried, called loved ones, and prayed for God's mercy and protection. Every time shots paused, I stood up to try and gain some sort of visual perspective on the source of the shots. But I didn't see a shooter, and I couldn't figure out exactly where the shooter was located. More fire erupted, and I ducked.

Casey and Heather had run from the spot we all had been dancing at minutes earlier. We knew Tracy was somewhere under the bleachers next to us, because we heard her voice. Chad wouldn't leave Nicol's side, staying behind with her when Michelle and I ran. I looked out across the moonlit venue and saw him hunched over her. His silhouette was among only a few still out in the open to protect or mourn loved ones. I was scared for him, but at the same time, so proud my best friend was brave enough to stay out in the open and refused to leave Nicol. He loved her, he really loved her.

Michelle and I needed to move again, in case the shooter—or were there several shooters?—was coming into the venue. I didn't want to stay fenced in if that were the case. We had to move toward the back of the venue, staying as close to the bleachers as possible for protection, then get behind the vendor booths and hopefully out of the confines of the concert area.

I leaned into Michelle's face, looked her in the eyes, and said, "I love you so much, baby. I promise we are going to get out of here." I didn't know for sure whether or not we were getting out of there, but I needed her to know I was going to do whatever I could to protect her. In some dark way, I was also taking that opportunity to say goodbye to her if that was going to be the outcome.

With the next break in fire, we moved toward the back of the venue, hugging the bleachers and vendor booths that lined the west side. Fire erupted, and we ducked behind a beer booth. Discouraged, I saw that the exit we were running toward was blocked by concert barricades. We sure as hell weren't staying in that venue, so we had to find another way out. People seemed to be escaping through the exit directly across from us on the east side of the venue. The problem was that we would have to run the length of a football field while completely exposed to the incessant gunfire.

I grabbed Michelle's hand, and we ran.

We jumped over bodies and chairs and around barricades and booths. My adrenaline was so high that my mouth was completely dry. It had sucked every bit of saliva out of my mouth, and though I felt like I couldn't breathe, I knew we had to keep going.

With some sense of relief, Michelle and I made it to that east-side exit where police officers stood guard with guns drawn as people shuffled past them. They directed us to run north toward the Tropicana hotel, so we followed some of the crowd that was going that way. For a short period, we were out of harm's way, although thoughts ran through my head that said otherwise.

I grabbed my phone—I had to call our parents. It was later, after 11:00 p.m., but there was a chance they would hear something on the news, so I needed them to hear from us that we were safe. I called my mother-in-law first, because she was staying with our kids. "Gloria," I said, "it's Ryan. I need you to know that Michelle and I are OK, but there has been a shooting at the concert we were at in Las Vegas. I'll call you again later, but know that Michelle and I are safe. We love you." I made a similar call to my mom.

A couple of police officers and Tropicana employees directed us into the back door of the hotel. We walked down to the employee cafeteria, where it looked like a war zone. Gunshot victims from the venue had fled to the area, and blood was all over the white floors and walls from people brushing up against them. People were screaming and crying.

As Michelle and I sat down at a small table, a loud crash caused everyone to completely freak out. Two young girls next to us pulled their table down on top of themselves, trying to gain protection in case something was happening inside the hotel.

My phone rang, and it was Chad. The connection was breaking up, but I heard him say, "Nicol is dead." Though we saw what we saw, a small part of us hadn't accepted the inevitable outcome. He said it again. "Nicol is dead."

I collapsed and started bawling. Michelle knew, and she too broke down. I thought, *How in the world were we singing and dancing with Nicol twenty minutes ago and now she is dead?* I was sick and in shock. I grabbed Michelle and held her tightly. While I was devastated by Nicol's death, I was relieved that Michelle was alive and by my side.

There was still so much chaos, so much fear, that collecting thoughts was all but impossible. We remained in survival mode since we had yet to hear the all clear from anyone. With every moment that passed, I couldn't help but wonder where God was in all of this. I knew he was with me. Deuteronomy 31:6 promises, "He will not leave you or forsake you," but I needed to see Him do something, with my own eyes, if I were to feel any real comfort.

Minutes later, a few hotel employees came to tell us everything was clear. We had to vacate the cafeteria and go up through the main hotel entrance. Still, nobody knew exactly what had happened, who had been shooting, and whether or not it was actually over yet, so we got up and walked out with lots of fear and hesitation. No more than thirty seconds after we got outside to the valet area of the Tropicana came another loud crash, and someone shouted, "Shooter!"

We ran back inside the casino and hid behind a bar. Sitting on the floor, we were able to assess the damage to the casino. Apparently, when the gunman started shooting into the concert venue, people in the Tropicana freaked out and ran. Someone outside the casino heard the gunshots and ran inside to announce it to everyone inside. Blackjack tables and slot machines were flipped over, signs were broken and flung throughout, and even personal belongings like purses and shoes were left behind.

We didn't know what to do or where to go next. A few televisions in the casino showed the news reporting the incident, but the information was all over the place and saying there could be multiple shooters. Even later after the lone gunman was found dead, the news continued to report the possibility of more shooters. We didn't have a moment to rest.

At some point, the hotel staff instructed us to make our way to the bottom floor of the casino through huge hallways to a convention center-like space. One by one, we were frisked and moved into that area. I guess they didn't want to take any chances that someone might be armed. Thoughts ran through my mind that we were under terrorist attack and, at any minute, the hotel we were in or even the whole strip might be bombed in a second wave of attack.

Peace finally came as fully dressed and armed military walked down the halls. In my opinion, there is no stronger defender than the United States military, and they were there to protect us.

Hotel staff walked the halls to let us know we were on lockdown and could be for a few hours. Staff brought us pillows and sheets so we could attempt to get comfortable. Michelle and I sat, and then lay down, on the hallway floor. I tried to close my eyes but couldn't. Every time I did, I saw people running, people bleeding, and dead bodies lying on the asphalt. It didn't help that wounded people in the halls were screaming and crying, making it feel like the war zone had followed us.

"Babe, look at my hat," Michelle said. "I think something hit it."

A small hole in Michelle's trucker hat looked a little like a burn mark, but my exhaustion combined with the desire to de-escalate caused me to shake it off. "Aw, it's probably nothing, baby. Don't worry about it."

Michelle rested her head back down on my lap, and together we restlessly waited it out.

After 4:00 a.m., the lockdown was lifted and we were given the OK to leave. We were told we could go back to our hotels as long as we weren't staying at Mandalay Bay, because the shooter had been in the Mandalay. Thankfully, Chad, Tracy, Heather, and Casey were staying at the Luxor, so Michelle and I grabbed our personal belongings and walked over to their hotel.

Being reunited with our friends was bittersweet. It was amazing to see the four of them, but one was missing and she would never make it back. Chad was lying on the bed when we walked in. He seemed numb but heartbroken. I climbed onto the bed, hugged him, and bawled. He hugged me back, but I could tell he had little left in him to give.

"I am so sorry, man," I said through tears. I was devastated, because I knew how much he loved Nicol. He would never be able to tell her that again. We all cried over and over again. We had been through hell, and it was still raw.

I picked up Michelle's hat. I wanted to see, with some clarity of mind, what had happened to it. As I turned it toward the front, I saw that a round of ammunition had not only hit the crown of that trucker hat but also had passed right through it.

"Holy shit, a round of ammunition went right through your hat," I said to Michelle. Without even knowing it in the throes of the chaos, I came that close to losing her on the venue floor. I was sick to my stomach, but I held it in to ensure I kept her as calm as possible. *My life would have been ruined. How could I ever explain something like that to our two daughters?* I grabbed Michelle and hugged her so tight to me.

I called my dad, and thankfully he answered on my first attempt to reach him. "Dad, Michelle and I are OK, but a shooting happened at the concert we were at in Vegas." He was in disbelief, but I could count on him to be strong and even-keeled as I explained some of what was racing through my mind, including the new discovery of nearly losing my wife.

At around 9:00 a.m., Michelle and I were able to get back into our room at Mandalay Bay. We packed our bags as fast as we could and headed down to the valet to get our car.

While Michelle and I were grateful to be on the road, we were facing a four-hour drive home and that felt like an eternity when all we wanted to do was see our girls. I drove as fast as I safely could, and we literally ran into the house to hug and kiss the girls. It was such a relief to be back in our house with our kids, far away from the recent darkness of events.

After we hugged and kissed the kids, and did the same to my mother-in-law, we had to break the news to them about what happened. I had to look my oldest, Alexis, in the eyes and let her know that, unfortunately, her Auntie Nicol had been shot and didn't make it. She broke down, crying in disbelief and pain.

Both my kids loved Nicol, and her absence would immediately leave a gaping hole in our framily.

POST-TRAUMATIC REALITY CHECK

The first few days home were difficult. A bowl dropping to the kitchen floor or a door unexpectedly slamming caused my heart to stop and my mind to reel. *What's going on? Is something wrong?* Anytime I had a moment of silence by myself, I replayed scenes of ducking underneath gunfire and running for safety. I didn't dare close my eyes during the day because the newly tattooed images behind my eyelids were war zone-esque. Falling asleep was a brutal task of the will, and just when it seemed I was finally sleeping, I would enter into a nightmare that looped every freaking moment of the traumatic event. I often woke up in a sweat, struggled to fall back to sleep, and then ended up back in the nightmare.

I tried to will away the trauma. I'd developed a strong enough will to do that before, and I could do it again. I also convinced myself that if I just kept positive and happy thoughts, if I laughed about other things when people were around, the painful wound would heal over.

On top of dealing with my hurt, and Michelle's pain, I was managing an outpouring of support we received. It might sound odd, but truthfully it was a lot to handle. We were surely blessed to have so many caring friends and family check in on us and bring meals. But we could only tell our story, explain the emotions, or accept encouraging words of "it will get better" so many times before just wanting to be alone so we could process our pain.

Michelle and I sometimes recalled moments from that night, and other times we tried to focus on anything but that. We also stayed closely connected to Chad, Tracy, Casey, and Heather. We texted and talked multiple times daily, and visited in person as often as possible. It was important for us to express how much we loved one another and our thankfulness that we made it home.

CNN, Fox, and *People*, as well as local media outlets, quickly bombarded us with inquiries. It's crazy how resourceful journalists are when it comes to getting personal information, whether a work phone, cell phone, or even home address. They all fought hard to get the best angle on the story, and I understood. Their job was to report this news of the largest loss of life in a mass shooting in US history, so the attention was massive. I tried to be gracious with anyone who reached out, but I could not afford that grace to the few who attempted to twist in a conspiracy theory. It wasn't the time or place for that shit.

Every reporter asked the same questions: "How are you dealing with things?" and "What was it like to be in the middle of the shooting?" I personally rejected a few, but I often talked to them because, while I didn't care to answer those questions, my friends and I cared deeply about telling Nicol's story. We wanted the world to know just how amazing she was and how devastating her loss would be.

We held a candlelight vigil and eventually a celebration of life. We made every moment as much about Nicol as possible and tried to be positive, because that's what she would have wanted and definitely what she would have done. Her smile always lit up the room. Without her, we all needed to smile to make up for the void.

Though we were absent a loved one, we committed from that day forward that we would never let the monster who took Nicol's life on October 1, 2017, rob us of the life we still had to live.

AN UNEXPECTED BLESSING: DEVELOPING THE WOUND-ANALYSIS FRAMEWORK

Some say the best way to regain sanity is to get back to a routine, and I agree. Two weeks after the Route 91 Harvest tragedy, I headed back to the office. Looking out my office window at the coast of Newport Beach, an overwhelming feeling came over me and with it, the question.

What in the hell am I doing with my life?

I would work through this question for nearly two years before it finally became the catalyst for my Wound-Analysis Framework. While I had some of the ideas and tools to process what I was going through after Route 91, the complete structure and method to analyze my wounds wasn't born until after my anxiety attack in 2019.

My past experience in working through transformational moments of life, as both a coach and pastor, led me to believe there was a much deeper question: *What is God doing through this season of my life?* I knew that answering my question would require more than what I was capable of on my own.

So, I prayed, asking God to reveal specifically what He wanted me to hear. I more diligently read His word to understand how He worked in transformational moments of my past. I also turned to others, including my wife, a few close friends, and my executive coach. Together we explored what had happened at Route 91 and, more important, why it happened.

Through these studies and conversations, I became confident that God was at work in my life through tragedy in the same way he worked through tragedy with Job. Job, a wealthy and righteous man, lost his children, possessions, and health. While Job's friends offered various explanations for his suffering, Job steadfastly maintained he had done nothing to deserve his misfortunes.

Just like my experience with the Route 91 shooting, the Book of Job does not offer a definitive answer to the problem of evil but rather invites us to trust in God's goodness and sovereignty. Even amid trials and tribulations, I am called to believe God ultimately works all things out for my good and His glory. The more I worked through what would become the Wound-Analysis Framework, the more clarity I was given to answer my "what" and "how" questions about this wound (and all of my others). *God, what are You doing through this wound? God, what do You want me to learn from this wound?*

As you review the framework that follows, and how I applied it to my wounds, I encourage you to apply it to yours. Please understand that the framework is less about understanding why the wound-inducing event happened (*How come that evil monster shot at us?*) and more about identifying the wound's existence, understanding how it impacted you, and finding ways to grow and become better because of it.

APPLYING THE WOUND-ANALYSIS FRAMEWORK

Acknowledge the hurt.

This wound related to violence and death resulted from losing a close friend in a tragic way, nearly losing my wife, and witnessing sights and sounds that are forever burned into my memory. The physical pain, and even the intensity of the emotional pain, lessens as the days go by. But the hurt remains every time we gather around the Friendsgiving table less one family member or attend another open-air concert in fear of what could happen. I admit the fear, because it is there. Denying it would be to deny the emotional reality I live with every day.

Realize the effect.

My Route 91 Harvest experience caused three major harms in my life:

1. My family, the close friend group I consider family, will never be whole again on this earth because Nicol is gone.

2. My mental health has suffered. I've lost many nights of sleep because, when I close my eyes, I am brought back to that night. As described at the opening of this book, I had my

first-ever panic attack approximately eighteen months after the event and have suffered several more since.

3. I nearly lost my wife and have had many nightmares about something happening to her in the future.

Unlock the greatness.

While the aforementioned effects have crushed me at times, God used the wound of violence and death to show me once and for all that healing my emotional wounds was the key to unlocking my greatness in these three ways:

1. Within my loving framily, there are always regrets, what-ifs and remember-when's. But the tragedy brought us closer. We realized how precious life is, how deeply we love one another, and how much we want to make every day together count.

2. The hit to my mental health influenced me to better prioritize my health, both in how much I strain my body as well as how I recover. I now understand the signs of anxiety and can often de-escalate the situation before it becomes an all-out attack. Having an anxiety attack also brought to light the seriousness of mental illness, leading me to speak about it more publicly. As a result, I have helped many others deal with mental illness battles.

3. While fear for my wife's safety has at times put me on edge in large public gatherings, it's helped me be better aware of my surroundings and more protective of her overall. Also, while I thought I could never love her more than I already did before the shooting started, I realized I had more love to give and, therefore, have given it.

Working through the prompts in the framework helped me lay a solid foundation for my life. I've gained clarity of my purpose, deepest passions, and non-negotiable principles. Building from that foundation leads to levels of personal and professional greatness that most people dream of but rarely achieve. While I hate what happened on October 1, 2017, I am grateful the tragedy of Route 91 became the catalyst for me to go deeper into my life and bring about the Wound-Analysis Framework.

The wound of violence and death wasn't my first wound, and it wouldn't be my last. To achieve my dreams and unlock the greatness inside of me, the greatness God created me for, I had to revisit my early life and apply the Wound-Analysis Framework to every wound I'd ever incurred, starting with my parents' divorce.

2

WOUNDED BY ABANDONMENT

CHRISTMAS 1983 WAS ONE OF THE BEST EVER BECAUSE I GOT my first motorcycle. I have a vivid memory of my dad running alongside me down the street. Like most dads, he was there to guide and protect me. Once he was confident I wouldn't fall, he stopped running and let me go on my own.

Less than one year later, my dad left me on my own, but this time, it wasn't to learn to ride a Suzuki JR50—it was to grow up and figure out how to become a man without him.

WANTING WHAT I COULDN'T HAVE

"Daddy still loves Mommy, but it's better for us to not be together." I was six years old, and that's about the only explanation I got of why my parents divorced, probably because it's all I could understand—though, I still couldn't really understand that. I later learned my parents often fought about how to live their lives. Their marital discord wasn't extremely dysfunctional or deeply philosophical. My dad was set in his ways and wouldn't budge for anyone. My mom was stubborn and didn't let up when she wanted her way. Conflict has a way of causing people to run for the hills instead of enduring to the finish line.

It was 1984. Apparently, the divorce had been some time in the making. My parents weren't getting along, and my dad decided it was better to bolt. But he didn't leave only my mom. He left me and my brother, Cory, too.

Making sense of my parents' divorce at age six was nearly impossible. *Why did he leave? And maybe more important, if God is against divorce, why would he allow my parents to get one?* While the church was kind to my mom in the aftermath of the divorce, this event was the beginning of my walking away from the religion I was raised in.

I definitely felt my dad's absence, both in his not being around physically every day and also in my mom's challenge to solely provide everything my brother and I needed. Without my dad, my mom had to start all over again. She hadn't worked a paying job because she was raising two kids at home. My dad cut up her only credit cards when he left.

To make matters worse, my dad wanted my mom to buy him out of his half of the house. The problem for her—us really—was that she had no money in her name. She hadn't socked away an "in case of divorce" savings account, so she was back at zero. My mom didn't want to give up that house we grew up in, the neighborhood where our friends (like Chad) lived, and the area where we attended school. Thankfully, my grandpa lent her the money so we could stay in our home.

My mom went right to work, so our home situation instantly changed. My brother, age three, and I were too young to care for ourselves so we were in full-time daycare when not in school. My mom did her best, but weekdays in particular were always chaotic: Up in the morning, off to daycare and school while mom went to work, picked up from daycare at the latest possible moment as mom rushed from work, dinner, homework if we had any, showers, and bedtime. The emotional, mental, and physical anguish must have been nearly unbearable for my mom, but she persevered for us.

Early on, my mom was working hard for us just to have basic necessities. Cory and I grew up on brown-label Stater Bros. mac and cheese, hot dogs, bread, milk, generic cereal, and other simple foods. My mom sometimes went without much food so we could eat. On the rare occasion we got new school clothes, it was one or two new items from Kmart.

As a kid, I didn't completely understand what I was missing. But occasionally, I noticed what my friends had and realized we couldn't have it. They had cable TV. We didn't. They got new clothes throughout the year. We didn't. They ate out and went on trips. We didn't.

Eventually, my dad moved in with his girlfriend, Madeline, and my brother and I visited them every other weekend. I will never forget the first time we drove up to his new house. It was a really nice house, and Madeline's boys were outside playing on their basketball hoop. It all felt so surreal. On one hand, I was excited to be with my dad. On the other, I felt some resentment when I realized our life was so much different. They had cool stuff, but we didn't. They were a big happy family, while we were alone with mom struggling. But because I was six, visiting there was also really cool. We had more family members who embraced us, and we enjoyed most of the same activities they did. We got to eat out, go on trips, ride dirt bikes in the desert, and enjoy a much nicer lifestyle.

As a young kid, I loved it all. But it magnified what we didn't have at home with Mom. I was so confused. A broken marriage created such seeming disparity. All of that enjoyment at Dad's made it hard to go back to Mom's—to what felt like less, or in some cases, nothing.

My first really bad decision as a young boy stemmed from what I believe was wanting what I couldn't have. It's not an excuse, but it's my reason. The wounded often wound others.

I was ten years old. By that time, my dad had married Madeline and, along with a new stepmom, Cory and I also gained three stepbrothers. Scott, Aaron, and Brian were a few years older than we were, but we all got along about as well as five boys can. My stepbrother Brian had gotten a new Nintendo race car video game, and we had so much fun glued to that TV all weekend. On Sunday, Cory and I were packing up to go back to Mom's. I wanted to keep playing that game. We had Nintendo at home, but we didn't have any cool new games.

So, I took that video game home with me—I stole it. I have no idea what I was thinking, because it wasn't as if my stepbrother wouldn't miss his brand-new game. No one would have believed it disappeared on its own, but I guess ten-year-olds aren't always the best decision-makers.

Shortly after getting home, I had a call from my dad. After denying to my dad multiple times that I had taken it, I finally confessed. "Why?" my dad asked. He was so disappointed that I would do that, and I get it. But I wanted the video game, and my mom couldn't afford to buy me one. She was too busy making sure we had enough macaroni and cheese to last another week. This was frustrating and confusing. I don't know if I was mad at my dad then, but the wound was growing and one day that hurt of being without would make itself known.

Nothing I could have said would justify the wrong I did. So, I just cried and said I was sorry.

Experiencing cool stuff at my dad's house didn't get any easier to process. Multiple times he told us we couldn't take our new Christmas or birthday gifts to our mom's house. We had to leave our gifts to enjoy at his house when we returned a few weeks later. I am not sure if my dad wanted to spite my mom or if it was his way of making his house more attractive. If it was spite, it made no sense. Sure, she frustrated him, but he was the one who chose to leave. If it was to make his house more inviting so we would want to be there, it worked only temporarily and caused far more long-term emotional damage.

Regardless of his reason for leaving, I regularly felt the sting of my dad's absence: Getting tucked in every night by only one parent. Feeling I didn't have a protector if we heard a noise outside. Playing catch in the front yard with someone else's dad. *Damn it!*

BAD REPLACEMENTS

Other men temporarily coming into my life and attempting to be my dad did far more harm than did good. I always did my best to accept and respect them, for the sake of our family and the good of my mom. But each relationship was simply another opportunity to be abandoned, for my mom to be hurt, and to have to tape off my wounds and fight for myself all over again.

To provide male influence for me and Cory, coupled with what I am sure was a need for companionship, my mom made a few attempts to bring a new man into our lives.

Jimmy was Mom's first attempt at a post-divorce relationship. He was quite a few years younger than my mom, and he had no kids. I thought it was so cool that he raced motorcycles, and he had a street bike he rode me on from time to time. He was a lot of fun to be around, and he was pretty good to my mom.

But being somewhat younger than she was, he was still hanging on to the party lifestyle. He drank quite a bit, but I don't remember it being a problem around the house. I think it happened more frequently when Jimmy and Mom went out. More than anything, the guy was not completely ready to give up his youth and take full-on responsibility in life.

One night, Jimmy left on his street bike to get milk from the local 7-Eleven just a few blocks away. Within minutes, we heard sirens in the neighborhood. Apparently, on his way back with the gallon of milk strapped to the gas tank, he rode a wheelie right in front of a police officer through a major intersection. Instead of stopping when the officer hit the flashing lights, Jimmy sped off. He led officers on a high-speed chase through our community until a police car shot out in front of him. His bike hit the patrol car, flipped end over end, and threw Jimmy to the pavement. Jimmy was taken into custody, admitted to the hospital to treat his injuries, and then booked in the local jail.

A couple of months after that incident, Jimmy disappeared, seeming to have fallen right off the face of the earth. My mom picked us up from daycare, and when we got home, Jimmy was gone. We all were confused and scared. We loved him and wanted to know he was safe. His car, his clothes, and even his wallet were still there. My mom called the police and eventually hired a private investigator. Foul play was doubtful. More likely was that he wanted to run away from the legal problems he was about to face.

Jimmy the fun-loving guy was there one day and gone the next. We were back to fending for ourselves.

Blake was my mom's second attempt at a post-divorce relationship. Blake would be my mom's first remarriage. With Blake, it seemed we were finally going to have a complete family. It was such a relief to know we would again have structure, stability, and provision. He had a family, and we blended pretty well. We did holidays and events together with both sides of the family.

But Blake also had a problem with alcohol. His wasn't so much partying as it was just evening drinking. And while Jimmy had turned his alcoholism into stupidity, Blake turned his alcoholism into anger and abuse.

Growing up my brother, Cory, had some behavior issues. He wasn't much different from other young boys, but he always found his way into some sort of trouble, mostly at school. Lots of defiance with his teachers provided him a permanent seat in the school office. Blake did not handle my brother's challenges very well. He once hit my brother so hard that he knocked him to the ground, cracking Cory's head open. In hindsight, I wish I had been older so I could have beat the shit out of him right there.

But I couldn't. So, my mom did the next best thing. She kicked Blake out of the house and, shortly thereafter, divorced him.

Then came Dana, mom's third relationship attempt and second remarriage after my parents' divorce. Dana started off like the others—a cool guy who really loved my mom. He had a solid job and drove a nice car, so we believed he would take good care of our needs. He also had a young son, and in my mind at the time, that meant Dana was a family guy. But there was definitely doubt in my head as I recounted the last two relationships—one disappearance due to immaturity and a forced-exit for abuse.

Dana came into our lives when I was in junior high and starting to push the envelope a bit. While I hadn't yet gotten into any real trouble, I was mouthy and defiant. I talked back to my mom and even broke a few minor laws with some friends. I guess that's a typical teenage boy. Combine my teen rebellion with Cory's ongoing antics, and Dana had himself a few parenting challenges as our new stepdad.

Parents are supposed to demonstrate level-headedness, responsibility, and maturity. Unfortunately, Dana lacked such qualities. His anger often got the best of him, and he sometimes came too hard at us.

One time he was yelling at me, I was yelling back, and he threatened to punch me in the face. We were chest to chest. At fourteen, I really couldn't have taken him on, but I shoved him out of the way. He pushed me into the wall and held me there with his forearm, choking my neck. Not too long after that, he and my mom split, and we were back to being a lonesome trio. It was such an interesting feeling, because I was grateful to have that asshole out of the house, but I was also immediately aware that we were on our own again with nobody else to provide for us or protect us.

A GOOD ONE AT LAST

Finally, my mom met Tom. I was seventeen, and my brother was fourteen. It didn't take long to see Tom was a great guy. He was kind, considerate, and honorable. He rarely spoke ill of others and respected those around him. He worked very hard and was successful. He had three kids—two lived out of state, and he shared custody of the third, who was local.

When my mom and Tom got married, I was so happy because I felt he was the one. I just knew he was the man to finally take care of my mom and be there to support us. Sure, he had past baggage. But he seemed to own his mistakes, and as far as I could tell, he was doing everything he could to grow from his hurts and become the man he desired to be. Part of his growth would be with us, and he was in it for the long haul.

Tom's challenge was that he came into our lives when both my brother and I were at the height of our troubled times. We'd had such instability for so many years, had far too long of a leash to take advantage of our mom, and were in our angsty teenage years. I was hanging around a very bad crowd, getting into fights, doing drugs, drinking a lot, and having many run-ins with the police (more on this stage of life later).

My brother was doing much of the same, less the fighting part of it, but he took run-ins with the police to a greater level. Without getting into too many details for the sake of his privacy, let's just say he made a bad choice to be the driver for a home burglary and took the brunt of the legal ramifications. Poor Tom had never experienced that type of stuff with his kids. Maybe they weren't like that, or perhaps he didn't see them enough to realize it. Nevertheless, this was new for him.

My mom and Tom fought early on about my brother and me. She often gave in to us, and Tom wanted her to more strongly stand her ground. She was definitely too lenient. I think she felt guilt for what my brother and I had been through, so she felt it was right to not be so hard on us. I respected Tom in that he never called my mom a bad name nor got physical with us.

Tom never attempted to replace my dad, but he saw what I was missing and did everything he could to show me how to be a good man. He wanted me to honor my mom, respect authority, be trustworthy, and do right by others. I didn't always want to hear it as a young adult, but deep down I knew I needed it. I wanted to be like Tom, and I wanted to make him proud. He influenced me to be a far better young man then, and grown man today.

MOVING TO DAD'S

After my freshman year of high school, I decided to go live with my dad and stepmom in Huntington Beach. I wanted to get to know my dad better and spend more time with him and my stepmom. I also felt a change of scenery would be good for my growth and development.

It wasn't an easy decision. The thought of leaving all of my friends and enrolling in a new school partway through high school was scary. I was also terrified to tell my mom. Though we butted heads, we were very close. I felt sick every time I had to think about telling her. I finally mustered up the courage. She was heartbroken, and it was definitely an emotional conversation.

The next year and a half had some memorable moments and lots of blurs: New school. Attempts to make friends. Trying out for athletic teams. It was way harder than I had thought it would be. Thankfully, playing high school basketball and baseball helped a little bit. But the new friendships never went too deep.

On the plus side, I got closer to my dad. I never actually knew what it was like to have my dad around a lot, so I loved seeing him every day. He attended most of my games and helped me with homework when I needed it. I got really close with my Madeline, too. We spent a lot of time together, and I loved being around her. She helped me get my driver's license and let me borrow her car from time to time until I got my own. She took me clothes shopping for school. We hung out after school and on weekends when my dad was working. We traveled east to visit my stepbrother Brian at college. And she took me to practices and showed up for every single game. This was what I had hoped for—and more—when I chose to move. The benefits seemed to make up for so much of the hurt I had experienced up to that point in my life.

But even the calmest seas experience storms, and storms were brewing. My dad, having had a strict upbringing coupled with his being a former police officer, was very strict himself. It was his way or no way. He expected nothing but A's and an occasional B on my report card. Anything less warranted punishment. When I got my first C, in honors chemistry, he took my car away even though I pleaded that I had tried my hardest. He was also very strict about how I acted and spoke. If I stepped out of bounds, I felt it, physically. There were no verbal warnings, just a whack across the back of the head. If I complained about the whack, I got another one.

It felt very much like the Catholic religion we were a part of—not the physical stuff, but the instant punishment and necessary penance for wrongdoing. Where was the grace? I didn't hear much about it on Sundays at mass, and I didn't feel it much from my dad during the week. I wasn't used to that, because my mom was pretty chill. In some ways, the stricter household was good for me. It gave me structure at a time when I was beginning to push boundaries, and it drove me to strive for excellence and not mediocrity in all that I did. But it was also a huge adjustment that felt damn near impossible to live up to at times. Could I ever be good enough?

The more my dad pushed, the more I turned to run in the other direction. Not only were his standards hard to live up to, but most of the time I didn't want them. Early in my junior year, especially after I got a car, I often went back to my mom's house in Yorba Linda, which was about twenty miles away. I headed there every weekend. Even when I had to work weekends, I drove back and forth between my shifts. I spent lots more time with my old friends and began dating a girl I really liked. In all honesty, I also liked the freedom I had when I was at my mom's.

I realized how much I missed my friends, my old school, and my mom. I saw what I had put her through by leaving, and I felt remorseful for it. I had abandoned her, just like what had been done to us ten years earlier. It tore her heart out. Gosh, it's even awful to type those words now. I had left upkeep of the house to her and my younger brother. I had, in some small way, disregarded all she did in my life to that point. We were a team. We'd been to hell and back together, and I wanted to be reunited with her and my brother, Cory.

Nearing the halfway point of my junior year, I wanted to move back in with my mom. It was getting way too hard to leave there on the weekends, and it felt painful to be away from there during the week. One night, in particular, was beyond painful. My mom had purchased an Anaheim Ducks ice hockey mini-package, so we got to go to a few games throughout the season. On the ride back to my dad's after a hockey game, my heart was hurting at the thought of leaving my mom. I couldn't bear it. I cried in the car on the way back to Dad's and then again when I got up to my room.

That was the first time I cried about being away from my mom and my friends, but it wasn't the last. The pain was becoming unbearable, but I was so scared to say anything to my dad. I was afraid he would be angry and even punish me.

The pain of staying in the situation became greater than the reluctance to speak up, so I decided to tell my dad how I felt. One night while out to dinner I said, "I want to move back in with Mom."

I don't know what I expected my dad to say, but he took me by complete surprise. "No, you need to finish high school here," he said.

"But I miss Mom, and I miss my friends. I don't want to wait that long," I said to him.

"You will finish what you started here. Once you are done with high school, you can do what you want."

I knew he hadn't seen it coming. Not many parents expect their child to say, "I'm out." After being a weekend-only father for eight years, my dad probably felt very hurt at the thought of my leaving. I explained why I wanted to move, how sad I was, and how much I missed my friends, but he wouldn't budge. I was heartbroken. My dad had shut me down, and my broken heart wasn't going to be healed.

RUNNING AWAY

My dad telling me no didn't help my situation at all. I had come to the decision that I needed to leave, but my dad's stern words made it feel absolutely impossible. Defying him would be the end of my life as I knew it, but I had to make the move as soon as possible since I felt there was no way I could endure another year and a half. I had to figure out a way to get back home to my friends, my girlfriend, and my mom.

I decided to take matters into my own hands. My mom knew where my heart was, and she wanted to do whatever she could to support me. She was excited for me to come back home. I finally decided to run away.

I don't think I ever again brought the conversation up to my dad, but it wouldn't have changed a thing anyway. His mind was set... and so was mine. I was angry at my dad at that point, so I didn't fully consider his feelings, but I felt terrible about leaving my stepmom. We were close and talked about so much, but I couldn't tell her about my plan.

One Friday morning, after my dad and my stepmom left for work, my friend Kevin showed up at the house. The prospect of my dad, the toughest guy I know, coming home while I was preparing to leave, had me and Kevin scared out of our wits. I didn't know how Dad would react when he got home and found I was gone, but I knew it wouldn't be pretty.

Let me be clear here that never, ever have I feared for my life around my dad. He was never that way with me and never would be. But I was concerned about a serious ass-beating at seventeen years old and being in purgatory for the rest of my non-adult life. If, for some off reason, my dad or even my stepmom were to show up at the house, it would be game over. After packing up a few of my things, Kevin and I sped off like robbers in a getaway vehicle.

It sounds funny now, but I went into hiding at the home of my mom's friend. I couldn't risk my dad finding me at my mom's house, whooping my teenage ass, and taking me back to his house. Only my mom, her friend, and Kevin knew my whereabouts.

When my dad and stepmom came home from work that night, they paged me. I was too afraid to answer. They eventually called my mom, and she shared what I did. It wasn't an easy conversation for my mom, but she wanted to protect me, and she did.

In hindsight, my heart hurts for what my dad and stepmom went through. They came home to an empty house, which a day earlier was occupied by a son they loved so much. I'd left to go back to my mom, and for my dad, that felt like defeat. He lost me to her, again. Now, as a parent, I can't imagine how horrible that must have felt. But leaving was the right decision for me.

I didn't know God very well yet, but I believe he calmed my spirit. Though I was scared to leave, my heart felt settled with the decision. I could not have endured another eighteen months living under my dad's strict rule, but I wish I could have executed a less clandestine departure. I wish my dad and I could have together concluded what was best for me.

I'd spent my whole life trying to prove to my dad that I was good enough, and I was tired of it. But before I could feel like I was good enough, I needed to learn what "good enough" means.

APPLYING THE WOUND-ANALYSIS FRAMEWORK

I was a fairly skilled motorcycle rider for many years, because of the foundation my dad laid for me on Christmas Day 1983. I didn't have that same fortune when it came to becoming a good man. I grew up trying to figure that out for myself. Relational chaos, frustration over lack of provision, and nearly unreachable standards all led to one big mess.

    I continued trying to be the best I could, learning empathy and compassion from my mom, receiving good wisdom from Tom, and sifting through good moments with my dad. I processed some emotions over the years, but it wasn't until early 2019 that I would discover the Wound-Analysis Framework and completely heal from this wound. I know now that God, in His loving kindness, orchestrated all of this to draw me to Him, to show me He is my ultimate healer, provider, protector, and sustainer. If only I had turned to Him sooner...

Acknowledge the hurt.

This wound of abandonment was the direct result of my dad leaving when I was young. While I would see him every other weekend, the void in his absence was often too great to bear.

Realize the effect.

The wound affected my life in two major ways:

1. Without a consistent father figure, I had to figure a lot out for myself. It would have helped to have my dad around when I was doing mechanical work on my first truck, struggling in school from the distractions of partying, and learning the

girl to whom I lost my virginity might be pregnant by me or someone else. I often felt neglected and lost.

2. My mom struggled a lot to provide for us, often working two or even three jobs. That meant I didn't get to spend as much time with her as I would have liked, and a lot of my needs and wants were left unmet while most other kids my age seemed to have it all.

Unlock the greatness.

Although my parents' divorce was not ideal, I gained an amazing stepmom I love dearly and a stepdad who taught me to honor and respect others.

Meanwhile, because my mother had to struggle and sacrifice to provide for me and Cory, I learned to appreciate the simple blessings in life and to value people over material possessions. That lesson was learned in a twofold manner. First, I learned the hard way that no matter the effort I, my mom, or anyone else put in, life was the way it was and I needed to either accept it or struggle through it. Second, I learned by watching my mom struggle. Her life was so damn hard, as she worked multiple jobs, sacrificed her free time, and even sometimes her own food, for my brother and me, but she never complained or made us feel like a burden. If she could do it with joy, so could I!

God used the wound of abandonment to show me how to be a good man, husband, and father. This means being a provider, protector, and sacrificial leader.

1. As a provider, I will work as hard as I can, using the gifts God has given me, to earn as much as I can to provide everything for my family, from the basic necessities to the

most amazing experiences. I learned this from my mom and Tom, as well as my dad and Madeline. I saw them produce various types of fruit by working hard to give us what they could. But provision goes beyond tangible goods. While my dad worked hard and provided lots of cool stuff and experiences, I didn't have him around when I most needed him. Provision also means I am present for my family when they need me.

2. As a protector, I will be the first to shield my family from any danger that comes their way, to stand by them as they navigate life, and to help them stay firm in what God has called them to. My mom did her best to protect us, but to me as a young boy, nothing replaced having a strong dad in the home. For me as an adult, flight will never be an option.

3. As a sacrificial leader, I will set aside my wants and needs to provide for my family's. Like my mom did for me, I will do my best to put my wife and kids first, making sure they know everything I do is to serve and support them, even if it feels personally costly to me.

As mentioned earlier, these lessons did not come quickly or easily. My dad and I did not speak for nearly two years. A combination of fear, hurt, and anger kept me from reaching out or connecting. I was a teenage kid set on living my life my way, and though I moved back to my mom's house for the right reasons, I didn't have the emotional intelligence to separate that from the negative emotions I felt toward my dad.

Nobody could have convinced me of that then. Instead, my dad was now completely absent as I tried to heal my wounds by myself and without the proper tools. Those two years would turn out to be incredibly, and disastrously, formative to my life.

3

WOUNDED BY LIES AND LOSS

FOR MANY KIDS, CHANGING SCHOOLS CAN BE BRUTAL. THANKFULLY, going back to my original high school came with ease. All of my friends welcomed me back, and I had timed my move so I would start back at the beginning of a new semester. What I didn't plan for was a random interaction with someone that would blow up my plans for smoothly transitioning back to my old life, drive me to tell one of the biggest lies of my life, and cause one of the deepest wounds I have ever incurred.

As my mom walked with me into the office on my first day back to school, an old acquaintance, Ryan, was standing there. I had gone to elementary and middle school with Ryan. Though he was a year older, we used to hang out a bit, mostly riding BMX bikes together. Something oddly clicked when I saw him in the school office. We talked about what I was doing back, and he extended an invite to hang out with him and his group of friends from that day forward.

While I still hung out with my old friends on occasion, I spent far more time with Ryan and his buddies. I would say they were the coolest group of guys at school, and because they were all older, it felt good to be accepted by them. This was definitely connected to my earlier abandonment wounds and the need to find acceptance with anyone I could, especially a popular group. We quickly went from socializing at school to hanging out on the weekends, drinking, smoking weed, getting into fights—and, eventually, hooking up with girls.

LOSING IT

All of us guys were heading out for spring break 1995 to camp at Crazy Horse, a campground on the shores of Lake Havasu. If you are at all familiar with spring break in Havasu in the '90s, you know that was the place to be. On holidays, especially the week of spring break, Crazy Horse was filled with wild teenagers and young adults left to their own devices. Loud music played all day and night, cars cruised up and down the aisles to party with others and check out the opposite sex, and there was this feeling of absolute freedom in a setting absent of all authority. I know now that combining tons of alcohol and teenage boys with no oversight is a terrible idea, but at that stage in our lives, it was the greatest. I mean, what could really go wrong?

The day after we arrived, we were surprised by a carful of our girlfriends pulling up to the campsite. We were pumped because we always had fun with them so they would add to the already insane party at the campground.

The biggest surprise for me was that one of the girls almost immediately expressed interest in me. Her name was Janet, and she was kind of the ringleader of them all. Janet was a senior who had always been part of the popular crowd. I didn't know her super well, and I never thought she would like me as more than a friend.

Janet and I stuck by each other as we wandered the campground. We were doing cherry bombs—cherries soaked in Everclear grain alcohol—and pounding beers with complete strangers who became instant friends. As the night was winding down, Janet and I started making out. A virgin, I wasn't pushy about going any further than that. I had thought about it a lot and talked about it with previous girlfriends, but I'd never had sex and definitely didn't think we would end up there at the end of the night.

Janet had other ideas, and we ended up in the same sleeping bag together in the bed of a truck in the blazing heat at a dirty campground. I am sure liquor played a part, but we were both clearheaded as to what was going on. Later, Janet told me the girls spent the majority of the car ride up talking about who they wanted to hook up with and she claimed me. I hadn't planned out an elaborate way to lose my virginity, but I never envisioned it quite that way.

The rest of the trip was pretty much a blur. I am sure too much alcohol consumption had something to do with that. But more so, the pinnacle of my week in Havasu was being accepted into a world by a girl I never thought I had a shot at, and that took every bit of my focus and attention.

As the trip came to a close, Janet and I briefly talked about what would happen moving forward. She knew that shortly before spring break, I had started casually dating another girl, so she figured I would go back to her. We kind of chalked up the encounter to one crazy week at Crazy Horse and we'd leave it at that. We wanted to remain friends and were good with going back to the way things were.

A BIG SURPRISE AND A BIGGER LIE

The following week, life was pretty much back to normal. We were all doing what we had to do to get by in school and continued to party hard on the weekends. Janet and I easily went back to being friends, but we occasionally spent time alone together and often ended the night with kissing. I am embarrassed to admit that now, and a part of me felt terrible since I was dating another girl. It was cheating, and I didn't want to be a cheater. But something about Janet, and my relationship with her, drew me in. I am sure the sexual connection had something to do with it, but something deeper between me and Janet had yet to be explored.

Around late June or early July of 1995, Janet pulled up to my house. Walking up my driveway, she had tears in her eyes.

"I'm pregnant," she said.

"What?"

I couldn't believe those words had just come out of her mouth. She was eighteen years old, and I was seventeen. *How in the heck am I going to be a dad? How will I manage taking care of a kid? How will I provide? How can I finish school?* I said all of those things in my head but not to Janet.

"Are you OK?" I asked her.

She said, "Kind of, but I am not sure if it is yours or not."

Janet had slept with another guy about a month after our night in Havasu, so it was possible it was his responsibility instead. Partial relief came over me. *Maybe I can go on living as a kid. Maybe I don't have to figure out how to get my life together in a moment's notice.* Again, I didn't say any of it out loud, because that's not what Janet needed to hear.

"Have you talked to the other guy?" I asked.

"When I told him about this, he said he doesn't want anything to do with me or the baby even if it's his," she said.

I thought, *How could any guy do that?* Even though I was a young punk kid, I was brought up with some level of responsibility and maturity—not counting how I got into that situation. I was taught to do the right thing…and what came out of my mouth next was what I perceived as "the right thing."

"I'll be here for you," I told Janet. "Regardless of whose baby it is, I will be here for both of you. We can tell everyone the baby is mine, and nobody has to know any different."

I didn't quite understand what I was getting myself into. I was prepared to tell the biggest lie of my life to my family members, who had given everything for me. I deeply cared for Janet as a friend—probably more than just a friend—and I didn't want her to be alone with a child. Sure, she had a supportive family and other friends. But she needed a man by her side, and her baby definitely needed a dad.

I knew what it was like to not have a dad around all of the time, and I didn't want the same to happen to that child if I had anything to do with it. The lie didn't seem like such a big deal, because I was doing something good for Janet and her baby. But that lie, though from a genuinely good spot, was actually the effect of my previous wound of abandonment. That wound, still unhealed at the time, was causing me to wound myself (and others).

I went with Janet and her mom to the first official doctor's appointment. It quickly became apparent the baby wasn't mine. The dates of possible conception were more than a month apart, and the latter date lined up with Janet's projected due date. A blood test with the biological father later confirmed this.

We talked it over and decided to keep that to ourselves. We didn't want anyone to know the baby wasn't mine, with the exception of Janet's mom and her stepdad. They were the only ones who knew the truth but kept the lie going to protect their daughter and grandchild. It's sadly fascinating how self-justification and self-preservation cause us to wound others or further wound ourselves. I felt it was the right choice because it would save Janet from more hurt, and I was falling in love with her and the baby that was coming.

That decision meant that even my family believed that baby was 100-percent mine without question. My mom asked me point-blank, and I lied to her face. She probably would have understood had I told her the truth, but I was far too protective to take a chance. In hindsight, hiding the truth was a bad decision. But as teenagers trying to navigate adult matters, we felt it was the best decision for us and the baby.

The roller-coaster ride was crazy those first few weeks. I told my mom she was going to be a grandmother. I told my brother he was going to be an uncle. I told all my friends I was going to be a father. There was a lot of awkward celebration, and some concern, but mostly a lot of support that helped us believe we would get through it all. It was hard to conceal the truth, but because the baby would be treated as mine, I felt nobody had to know any different.

I had no idea how difficult being a father would be, and even less of an idea as to how much it would change, and even save, my life.

PROTECTING THE PROTECTOR

Getting into small-time trouble was the norm for our friend group, but every so often the trouble turned dangerous and even life-threatening. My friend Ryan was hooking up with a girl who had a crazy ex-boyfriend. Our group had a few mild encounters with his group, but nothing went too far because we were always in public places, until one night when we weren't.

One Saturday night we were all invited to a party at Ryan's girl's house in Chino. Janet came along, and she was pretty dang pregnant.

We pulled up to the house, surprised to find the ex-boyfriend there with a few of his buddies. Ryan jumped out of his truck and took off running after the guy, chasing him around the corner to another street. We all jumped out of our cars and went after him. As I ran around a car, a big guy clotheslined me and got me into the tightest headlock. His arm was across my face and neck, and in addition to my airway being cut off, my bottom lip was smashed into the braces on my teeth.

For some reason, he let up and let me go. My mouth bleeding and gasping for air, I ran down to the end of the street, where Ryan and everyone else was squared off and ready to fight. But the ex-boyfriend and his group realized they were outnumbered, so they took off.

Proudly, we all walked back to the house, talking about how we got over on them. We didn't realize at the time that cornering and outnumbering the ex-boyfriend and his buddies had made the situation far worse for our group.

An hour or so later, as we were drinking and dancing and hanging out back at the girl's house, the doorbell rang. Someone opened the door to a scene I will never forget—twenty or so guys standing in the front yard, holding pipes, chains, and bats.

There were only ten of us guys, and we didn't have any weapons at all. Someone threatened to call the cops, but because some of the guys I hung with never backed down from anything—you can call that pride, stupidity, or a bit of both—they said not to call the cops because they were ready to fight. The other group of guys proposed we meet down the street at Don Lugo High School, where we would all go at it.

Those guys took off, and we were set to follow. Janet lost her mind, crying because she knew what we were stepping into. Our group had no chance against the number of guys they had with them, and the fact that they had weapons meant someone, or all of us, would end up hospitalized or even dead. It was clearly a loss before we even got started.

"Don't go! You can't go," Janet yelled through her tears.

I heard her, but I couldn't listen to her, even though I was so scared.

I had been in a few small fights but nothing like what was about to happen. I hadn't ever been hit with a weapon like that and could only imagine how bad it was going to be. I pictured the scene between the Greasers and the Socials from *The Outsiders*: Fists flying, guys on the ground being kicked in the ribs, someone stabbed and bleeding out on the ground with no relief in sight. I couldn't imagine how painful that would be, and I didn't want to find out. I didn't want to be on the receiving end of such violence. I was pissed at my buddies for so pridefully speaking up, but I couldn't be the punk and leave them hanging. If one was going down, we all were.

We piled into two vehicles, including my truck, and headed over to the school. As we pulled in, the ex-boyfriend and his buddies were all there, spread throughout the parking lot. *Holy shit, we are going to fucking die*, I thought. Fear again came over me. I wanted to warn my boys, but I couldn't. Everyone hopped out of the bed of my truck and just as I was about to get out, my friend Ty approached me.

"Dude, you have to go back to my truck," Ty said, looking dead serious and stern.

"What? Why?" I asked, both puzzled and scared.

"I have a gun under the seat. Go grab it," he yelled.

"A gun—what?" I replied.

"Go! Go get it. Hurry up and get it, and come right back," Ty ordered.

I was scared, but this was the only way we were going to stop these guys from beating us to a bloody pulp.

I jumped into my truck and sped back to the party house. All my fear, coupled with the adrenaline of going to grab a gun, had my heart feeling like it might explode. I rushed over to Ty's truck to grab the gun.

"What are you doing?" Janet asked. I ignored her at first, but she wouldn't relent. "What are you doing? What are you looking for?" she yelled at me.

Knowing she wouldn't stop asking, I said, "A gun—Ty said he has a gun under the seat, and I need to grab it. It's the only way we are going to survive this."

Janet bawled even louder than before, yelling at me to stop. Of course, she was freaking out. Bringing a gun back to a fight already full of weapons would only worsen the conflict. I could barely fit my hand under the seat. It was dark, and I couldn't see anything. I felt around everywhere under that seat, but I couldn't find the gun. Honestly, I wanted to search all night so I didn't have to go back and get my ass kicked.

Either Ty was forgetful, crazy, or lying, but no gun was under the seat of his truck. After about five minutes, I gave up on the search and sped back over to the school. No more than ten minutes could have gone by, but the fight was already over. Some of my buddies were walking away from the school, while others were driving away. Torn clothes and bloody bodies, they were a mess.

Of everyone, Manny and Vinny got the worst of it. Manny had extreme pain in his ribs from being hit by a bat and was losing consciousness from a blow to the head. Vinny, bleeding heavily, had been hit in the head with a metal pipe. They had to get to the hospital, so I grabbed Vinny and put him in my truck while another friend did the same with Manny. I raced back to the house for Janet, and we drove one hundred miles per hour to the hospital.

On the way, I called the only person I knew would help without asking questions. "Mom, we were in a fight. Vinny is really hurt. He's bleeding from the head, and we need to get him to the hospital. You need to meet us there right now." My mom met us there and helped us get Vinny checked in. I have no idea what she told the hospital staff, but because Vinny was eighteen, they didn't need parental consent, so they took him in, stitched him up, and sent us home.

The next day, Ty came to my house to hang out in the driveway and tinker with our trucks as we did most days.

"Hey, man," he said, "there was never any gun under my seat."

"What?" I replied.

"I made it all up," Ty said.

"Why the fuck would you do that?" I asked.

"Because you had no business being in that fight. It was too dangerous, and you have a baby to support. I didn't want to risk you getting badly hurt, or worse," he said.

I hugged him and told him how thankful I was for him. Ty had protected me from what could have been so much worse than the busted lip I got. While we did a lot of stupid shit and got in loads of trouble, each of us always had the other's back, and that was some of the most evident proof I had ever seen in my life—talk about feeling accepted!

I am thankful to Ty for that, but in some weird way, it was actually God's providence that protected me. While I didn't at the time consider that God was present in my life, I now know He was acting on my behalf. God brought Janet and me together in Lake Havasu, and He drew us closer together when she got pregnant. God caused Ty to extend love and mercy to me on fight night because of Janet's pregnancy. God used that baby, by way of many precious moments and people, to protect me from being hospitalized, or worse, that night.

A FEW MONTHS OF JOY

The months leading up to the baby's birth were a blur. I was a seventeen-year-old dad-to-be who needed to quickly grow up and take the necessary responsibility. While her mom was incredibly supportive, I spent as much time with Janet as possible. The plan, at least in the near term, was for Janet and the baby to live with her parents while I stayed with my mom until we could afford to make a move. We did nursery prep, hosted a baby shower, and even went to Lamaze classes. I also tried to accompany Janet to every doctor's appointment.

I did all this while starting my senior year of high school. Though I was pretty much over school at that point, I needed to do well enough to maintain a decent GPA and graduate. People at school, students and staff alike, were all super supportive and excited for me and Janet. I was working a terrible telemarketing job, but I kept it because we needed to save up as much money as possible. My mom was behind me every step of the way. Things were great overall, especially considering the circumstances of having a baby as a teenager out of wedlock and without a good job.

In late January 1996, Janet went into labor. Being in the room as she gave birth was a surreal experience. I saw things you can never unsee. It was a crazy environment for a kid to be in. Despite what I'd previously seen on TV or in health ed, nothing could prepare me for witnessing a new life entering the world. I stood by Janet's side, holding her hand the entire time. I wanted her to know I wasn't going to abandon her.

As baby Jessie—her name is changed for privacy—came into this world, we rejoiced. Her little fingers were so dainty—ten of them... *check!* Her tiny toes with miniature toenails were so adorable—ten of them...*check!* Her cute little lips quivered as she felt the first rush of air outside the womb. Then she let out a cry far too loud for the little body it came out of, but she was announcing to us all that she'd made it.

"Do you want to cut the umbilical cord?" the doctor asked.

I looked at Janet and she nodded. "Sure," I hesitantly replied, not knowing what the heck to do.

The doctor handed me the scissors, showed what and where to cut, and I did it.

I was in love. How I could love Jessie so much so quickly, especially knowing she wasn't biologically mine, was mind-blowing. But I loved her with all my heart from the moment I laid eyes on her. No matter how crazy, or how hard, I was making a statement in that delivery room that I wouldn't let this child or Janet be abandoned in their time of need. Sure, others could step in, but I was taking responsibility. Nothing would cause me to take flight. My final commitment was my signature at the bottom of Jessie's birth certificate: *Father, Ryan James Miller.*

I am not sure how I managed to handle the pregnancy, birth, and first few months of that child's life. I am sure I freaked out a time or two, and Janet and I had some arguments along the way. It wasn't easy being teen parents, and it put stress on our relationship. But all in all, seventeen-year-old me was doing what he could to take on a role many adults fail at. I wasn't better than my dad, and I had a lot to learn, but I knew from my dad's leaving that abandonment hurts the family. I wouldn't choose to make that mistake.

Most people take flight when things get hard, in all aspects of life, including relationships, but I never thought about leaving Janet. I did not once think about cheating on her with another girl. As a matter of fact, going through the process of pregnancy, childbirth, and child-rearing with Janet brought us closer. In tough times, it's easy to walk away from a relationship if you don't have something holding you down. But we did, and it meant that when we hit rough patches, we had to work through it, for our good and Jessie's. Being in that relationship with Janet, and being a dad to Jessie, made me part of something far more meaningful than a high school fling, and it felt amazing.

After the baby was born, we kind of went back to a regular routine. Janet returned to her job, which was our primary source of income. I went back to school and had part-time employment. I needed to stay employed and keep up with my schoolwork . Janet continued living with her parents and I with my mom. We stayed together on occasion but not every day. It was hard to maintain a healthy relationship while taking care of the baby.

It also didn't help that I was still a kid. As much as I wanted to be responsible, I also liked to party with my buddies. Janet wasn't happy about that.

PROTECTED AGAIN

One night in June 1996, just after my high school graduation, my buddy JD called. He asked if I wanted to hang out with him and our other buddy, Manny. It was already fairly late on a Sunday, but because I didn't have school the next day, I was considering it. I was with Janet at her parent's house, and she heard the context of the invite.

"Absolutely not," Janet said. "You can't be out partying on a Sunday."

"Seriously?" I replied. "I will be fine."

"No," she snapped back. "No, you cannot. You are a dad now, and you have a responsibility to be with me and Jessie. You can't just go out whenever you feel like it."

I was pissed. I wanted to go out. I wanted to hang with my boys. For some reason, Janet was already a little on edge that day. Maybe the baby was being a challenge, or perhaps we had been arguing. I do not recall. But her emotion turned to a fit of sorts. She was crying and angry. She had snapped into an odd combination of protective momma-bear pleading for her baby and heartbroken child pleading for her own protection.

Begrudgingly, I obliged. I'd done so much to be the responsible grown-up in a serious relationship with a baby, and I just wanted a night out as an irresponsible teenager.

A few days later, my phone rang. "Ryan, it's JD."

"Dude, where are you? I haven't heard from you in a few days. Are you OK?"

"Manny and I got into some shit, and we are in Mexico," he told me.

"Mexico—what? What the hell happened? Are you OK?" I was freaking out a bit.

"I can't say much, just that something really bad happened last Sunday night. I don't know what I'm going to do."

I had not ever heard that level of fear in JD's voice. He was a tough guy and somewhat accustomed to sketchy situations. But this sounded different, and it was.

The news later reported that a casual hangout turned into a horrific scene in an apartment in Orange, California. Two people were in the hospital with gunshot and stab wounds. Manny and JD were suspects on the run.

After a few more days, I got another call from JD.

"I can't take it, man. I can't live in hiding in Mexico for the rest of my life. I need to come home and turn myself in." And that's what happened. JD drove back to the United States and turned himself in to local authorities. Manny also soon came back to SoCal and was detained.

I cannot go into the details of what happened or what I heard, but after a long trial process, both were convicted on multiple counts from the events of that night. Manny went on to serve more than eighteen years in prison, while JD served fifteen. You may wonder why I won't share more. I know private details that were not fully, publicly disclosed, and I am choosing to hold those to my grave. Both friends were punished and did their time, and for me, that is enough.

It is not lost on me that I was once again protected by my decision to stand by Janet. Committing to Janet and supporting Jessie may seem selfless. "What a good guy," some say. But the decision I made on my driveway years prior may have benefited *me* more than anyone else.

THE DEEPEST WOUND

My decision to be a father to Jessie and partner to Janet may have twice protected me from devastation, but unfortunately, it couldn't protect me from the reality that Jessie might never really be my child. The chances of my relationship with Janet lasting were slim from the get-go, but its ending proved to be one of the most difficult ordeals in my life. We both were struggling to manage life, relationship issues, and parenthood.

We were just kids. We didn't have the proper tools to deal with the day-to-day frustrations. While we loved each other very much at certain points in our relationship, that love was fading. Janet told me she couldn't do it, do us, anymore. I didn't take it well, but

I eventually got over the fact that Janet and I wouldn't be together any longer. But the breakup isn't what cut me the deepest.

At first, even though I was no longer her boyfriend, it seemed Janet would still let me be the daddy to Jessie. After all, I'd spent two years as Jessie's dad, changing diapers, going to doctors' appointments, seeing her take her first step, and even hearing her call me "Dada." It was amazing to be a part of her life and watch her grow. Sure, it was hard, but it was well worth it! I had no plans for that part of my life to ever end.

Since I'd been a staple in Jessie's life, involved every step of the way, Janet and I decided I would continue to see Jessie. We worked out a visitation schedule that had me taking Jessie during a couple of days a week when I wasn't working. I mostly hung out at home on the days I had her, playing with her, cuddling with her, and loving on her. I honestly wish I could relish more memories. Due to the trauma blacking them out, or God graciously allowing me to forget them and reduce the pain, I struggle to remember much about those days.

It was hard going from seeing her almost every day to only one or two days a week, but I loved Jessie and wanted to be around her. I wanted to make sure she had a dad around to provide for and protect her in the best ways I could.

Aside from visitation, I agreed to pay Janet money every month to help her out. I was working only part time, so it wasn't much, but when it comes to young parents with a baby, everything helps. I wanted to live up to my commitment to stand by Janet and support her. It wasn't easy, because I needed money for my own stuff and wanted the freedom most teenagers do. It made it harder to date new girls, but it was worth it. It fulfilled me to be present and give care—two factors I missed from my dad while I was growing up. I knew in my soul it was the right thing to do.

One day, Janet wanted to talk. "This isn't working. I don't want to keep this up anymore," she said coldly.

"Keep this up? What are you talking about?" I replied.

"Jessie. It's time that you stop seeing her."

I broke down crying. I couldn't believe what I was hearing. After nine months of pregnancy, and two and a half years of life with Jessie, Janet wanted to end it all. "Please, don't do this," I said. "Please, don't take her away from me."

But nothing got through to Janet.

Being told this was the end of my role as Jessie's dad was by far the most hurtful thing I had experienced up to that point of my life. I just kept crying. I loved that baby so much, and I couldn't imagine my life without her. Logically, it made complete sense. She wasn't mine biologically and there were no future plans for Janet I to be in a relationship. That could surely cause future confusion and hurt for Jessie. I argued with Janet. I begged her to change her mind. But in the end, the decision was hers. I had no control over what was happening. As much as I wanted to fight for as long as I could, Janet was right. This was best in the long run for Jessie, for Janet, and for me.

I couldn't hide my pain, not even for a day. As I picked myself up off the driveway from the emotional beatdown I'd just taken, another painful reality hit. I had to tell my mom, family, and friends I had lied about fathering Jessie.

I walked into the house, dejected, and shared with my mom the conversation I'd just had with Janet. My mom was beyond devastated, expressing deep sadness for the loss as well as anger with Janet for her decision. In the moment, Mom's grief of losing Jessie overpowered any potential for her to be mad at, upset with, or disappointed in me. My mom later shared that while she was upset with me for lying that whole time, she was proud that I'd voluntarily stepped into that role and for the reasons I did it.

Other family members also took it hard. They had grown to love Jessie. She had been part of our family.

APPLYING THE WOUND-ANALYSIS FRAMEWORK

I would have never imagined that my worst lie, though told with good intention, would cause one of the deepest wounds of my life. It was a lesson I had to live and learn. While there was some short-term embarrassment in owning up to my lie, I didn't care about that. I cared about the baby. I was present when she was born, said her first word, took her first step, and first called me "Dada." I cannot erase that from my memory. Eventually, the hurt went away. I slowly saw that the most difficult season of my life so far ended the best way it could have for all involved.

Acknowledge the hurt.

The self-inflicted wound of lies and loss was birthed from my abandonment issues. It was a well-intentioned desire to love and care for another human, or two, but the joy it brought me was only temporary.

Realize the effect.

I was heartbroken after that little girl was erased from my family's life. Someone else I loved was taken from me. I tried to fill the hole left in my heart with quick fixes like one-night stands and self-medication, but those created new wounds and further exposed this meaningful one.

Unlock the greatness.

God used my bad decisions for good during that season of my life. He used the wound of lies and loss to strengthen me in two ways:

1. Acting as a father to that little girl was a blessing to me on so many levels. I learned some of what it means to be a dad, and I was forced to grow up when most boys my age were completely immature.

2. My role as a father figure also protected me from harm. If not for Janet telling me not to go out with my two buddies in 1996, I too would likely have fled to Mexico and returned to face a prison sentence.

Having sex before marriage was a mistake, as was lying about the child being mine. But God, in His kindness to me far before I surrendered my life to Him, provided a very unexpected hedge of protection over my life. If He hadn't, my life likely would have taken a very different turn.

While I am so grateful for God's mercy during that time, although I wasn't ready to accept it. Instead, I continued trying to tape up the wounds while creating new ones in the process, particularly when it came to sex and relationships.

4

WOUNDED BY SELFISHNESS AND SEX

INSTEAD OF LEARNING FROM MY RELATIONSHIP WITH JANET—AND the bad choice to have sex far too early in life—I further opened that wound and allowed it to destroy so much more of me.

Rolling into summer 1998, I was six months out from turning twenty-one and eager to take my party lifestyle to a whole new level. Janet was in the rearview mirror, and I was laser-focused on "making up for lost time." I felt I had wasted prime years of my life when I could have been sleeping with lots of other girls.

My best friend Kevin and I were thick as thieves. He got kicked out of his house for partying too much, and because my mom was so chill, she let him stay with us. We worked at Circuit City, and when we weren't working, we were out partying. We hit the club and bar scene from Orange County to Los Angeles six nights a week, often joined by other guys and girls who were friends. We were having so much fun but partying way too hard—mostly alcohol and some select drugs. I got to know most of the club promoters, so we had VIP connections almost everywhere we went. If I didn't have a hookup, I usually talked my way into the VIP area anyway.

On the dating scene, I did all I could to make up for that lost time. Whether I met a girl on the dance floor or was introduced by a friend, if she was attractive, I tried to hook up with her.

My success rate was far better than average. It felt good to be desired by other girls. Definitely an ego boost, it was also a mere temporary fill of the gap left by my earlier losses. It's hard for me now to claim I genuinely respected those girls, because if I had, I would not have slept with any of them.

At the time, I always tried to treat the girls respectfully, whether that meant paying for their food and drinks, holding the door for them, or complimenting them. I'd lost any sense of sex as a meaningful exchange and had turned it into an opportunity to gain short-term pleasure. In hindsight, I sound like a complete idiot, but back then I thought it was so cool to hook up with girls like that.

STOPPED IN MY TRACKS

I met Michelle through a friend who had dated her for a couple of years. She fit right into the crew and hung around with us all the time. We spent time with car clubs at the local coffee shop, at parties in the area, and watching TV at home. While she was like one of the guys, she was also a beautiful girl with an awesome personality. Over time, she and I became pretty close friends. She never had to worry about me trying anything disrespectful on her, and from my perspective, she was a refreshing reprieve from my crazy party lifestyle.

Michelle and I talked about everything. I shared my war stories and dating struggles, and she talked about the ups and downs of work or issues at home. Eventually she shared with me that she and her boyfriend, who was my buddy, were having relationship problems. As a good friend to both, I listened and advocated for them to work through it. I can honestly say I always came from a good place and wanted to see their relationship thrive.

Around Michelle's twenty-first birthday, in June of that year, she called it quits. As we all know, breakups are rarely easy. I wanted her to know I supported her and that she was welcome to hang out with us all more often. She joined right in with our crazy schedule as though she were meant to be there all along.

One night in August 1999, we were out in a big group at a favorite club. We were drinking, dancing, and having a great time. A little bit of flirty dancing may have been happening between Michelle and me on the dance floor, but in the moment, we were just two friends letting loose. We all ended up back at our friend Justin's house for a bit and then decided to head home.

Lucky for me, home was right across the street. Michelle was in no shape to drive, so I invited her to stay at my house. It wasn't the first time she had stayed over, so it didn't seem a big deal. We always respected each other's boundaries, sleeping on opposite sides of the bed with no inappropriateness.

But something was different that night, and Michelle made a move. I don't know that I would have ever been the one to initiate a romantic advance—not because I didn't think she was beautiful. It just wasn't in me to cross that line with her and risk ruining our friendship that meant so much to me.

Reflecting back on that night, I see God at work. While he does not necessarily condone a sexual relationship outside of marriage, God still extends grace to us. In the Book of Genesis, before Satan tricks Adam and Eve to sin, they are walking around naked and without shame in the Garden of Eden. That's how it felt to wake up next to Michelle that next morning. There was no shame and no thought of a one-night-stand. Twenty-four hours earlier, I was a man on a hook-up mission. In an instant, I was stopped in my tracks by a woman from whom I'd least expected it. She didn't demand anything, but she was more than I had ever experienced before. She was one of my best friends, and that friendship was the foundation for something so much greater.

And while it was in some way explainable only by divine intervention, we knew it was the way things were supposed to be. It felt as if every moment of our lives had led us to that encounter—to give each other the most intimate and protected parts of ourselves.

TEMPORARILY BROKEN...AGAIN

Before Michelle and I started dating, I had given up on serious relationships. I had a few long-term relationships in my past but none had worked out. A couple of them broke my heart, and the most recent one was incredibly toxic. I had no intention of dealing with that again. I turned to randomly hooking up with girls. It was fun at the time and a great way to brag to all my guy friends. But, truth be told, the best part of hooking up with random girls was that I didn't have to get my heart broken again.

I had fallen in love with Michelle, and I wanted to be with her. But days after we connected, she called to tell me she wanted to break it off and go back to her ex-boyfriend.

I was devastated. I questioned her and faintly remember her telling me that because of their history she felt she needed to give it a shot. Later I found out she had felt so mentally and emotionally downtrodden over the course of their relationship that she didn't have the fight in her and just gave in to his pleading.

I definitely felt hurt, and I was angry with myself for letting my guard down. Michelle and I stopped talking altogether. It was so weird that just weeks prior we were best friends who talked daily and hung out routinely, but all of a sudden we simply didn't exist in each other's world. It was too awkward. Thankfully, that season did not last very long at all.

For some reason, my best friend Kevin and I were hanging out at our friend Justin's house, though neither Justin nor his parents were home. Kevin and I got hungry, so I ran to Del Taco to grab us some lunch. When I got back, I dropped the food on the counter and stepped into the bathroom to handle some business. I wasn't in the bathroom long before I heard raised voices in the kitchen. One voice was Kevin's, and the other was Michelle's ex-boyfriend. I couldn't figure out what they were arguing about, but then I realized he was looking for me. Kevin was trying to de-escalate the situation. I walked out of the bathroom and was confronted face to face.

"You and Michelle hooked up, didn't you?" her ex asked. "Just tell me. I know you did."

I knew he couldn't take the truth, and frankly, it wasn't his business. "No, man, nothing happened," I replied.

"I know you did!" he yelled. "Just tell me!"

"No, nothing happened. Chill out," I said. I backed up a step and postured toward the possibility of him throwing a punch. I had a feeling he would do something but didn't want to trigger him, so I didn't clench my fists or even put my hands up.

"Yes, you did. I know it!" he yelled again.

With that, he wasn't going to let up and we were on the verge of a fight so I told him it was better if we were out back. I really didn't want it to turn physical. We had too much history between us, and it would cause far too many other problems.

As soon as we stepped outside, he got back up in my face. He yelled some more, and then it happened. First, he grabbed an aluminum baseball bat that was in the backyard, as if he wanted to hit me with it. Thankfully, Kevin stepped out and grabbed the bat from his hands so he couldn't use it. He came toward me and took a swing. He missed and, when he did, I put him in a chokehold and took him to the ground, pinning him between the house and the pool deck.

"Chill out. You have to chill out, man," I said. "I will let you up if you promise to quit. Just leave." I wasn't going to let him go until he was willing to calm down. "You went too far, and for nothing. There's no reason for us to be in this position," I told him.

"OK," he said. "I'm good."

He got up, continuing to yell at me and call me names, and took off out the front door.

Kevin and I could not believe what had just happened. It was like a crazy nightmare had just played out. As our adrenaline settled, we grabbed our Del Taco bag, sat on the couch, turned on the TV, and ate our lunch.

Michelle's ex-boyfriend, meantime, sped over to her parent's apartment, where she was living. He busted into the front door and went after her, calling her names and threatening her in front of her parents.

In the midst of all the yelling, he commented that he had kicked my ass and left me bloodied at Justin's house. Michelle freaked out that I was hurt, somehow slipped past him to her car, and raced over to Justin's. Her ex chased her out the door, got into his car, and got back to my neighborhood before she did.

A huge argument blew up in the middle of my street, catching the attention of my stepdad, who was inside our house. Multiple people witnessed the chaos, all while I was eating Del Taco and watching TV in Justin's house.

As horrible as the day's events were, that was the final nail in the coffin for Michelle to realize she needed to break that relationship off once and for all. It had become very toxic, and she needed to be free of it. She and I discussed all that had happened between us, as well as all that had happened that day. I understood her decision to get back with him one final time, and I was willing to put it behind us. We knew the best thing for us both was to be together, so we became a couple.

GOING ALL IN

As much as I feel called to share my life through this book, this has definitely been the most difficult chapter to write. While Michelle and I are in an amazing spot in our lives, recalling some of the following memories reminds me it wasn't always the way it is now. Circumstances got hard, and ugly, and I'm not proud of that. But as is life, these experiences shaped me to be the man I am today. So here goes.

Michelle and I, both twenty-one at the time, began officially dating around August 1999. It was great to finally be together publicly, though not everyone was pumped on our news. That didn't matter, though, because those closest to us were super supportive.

A few months into dating, Michelle moved in with me and a few buddies. As crazy as it might sound, Michelle and I loved being together all the time and rarely fought. We just made sense together. Even in the midst of having roommates and people over regularly, we always found time to be alone together.

To this day, one of our best memories is that of our at-home date nights. We didn't have a lot of money, so we couldn't eat fancy dinners out (or in for that matter). Date nights involved enjoying chicken, pasta-roni, Pillsbury oven-baked rolls, and a bottle of Arbor Mist at our dining room table. It was our version of a fancy dinner date. It makes me laugh a little now, but more than that, it fills my heart that even then, we loved just being together and did what we could to make it happen.

As we neared our one-year mark, we entertained the idea of getting married. It made sense. We were best friends. We loved each other. And we wanted to be together forever.

In August 2000, I proposed. I would love to say I came up with an elaborate, romantic plan to propose to her, but I didn't. Wanting to look cool but being a bit nervous, I proposed across an Olive Garden table over salad and breadsticks. She was expecting the proposal.

Obviously, not that night—but she knew it was coming. She said yes without hesitation. We got a few claps and cheers from the restaurant, and we went back to chowing down breadsticks.

On March 18, 2001, I married my best friend. We wrote our own vows, and I meant every word of mine. I wish I had saved them so I could recite them now. But my vows were sincere. I loved Michelle so much and couldn't imagine marrying anyone else, ever.

Our closest family and friends were there, and we partied so hard—drinks flowing and the dance floor bumping. I chose "You're the Inspiration" by Chicago for our wedding song. To this day, when I hear Peter Cetera open with lyrics of love that's meant to be and lasts forever, I get tears in my eyes, thinking of how God perfectly brought me and my wife together to love each other forever.

...Even though we later tried to screw it up.

A JOYFUL START

I often joke that if Michelle had to take one pill per day to survive for the rest of her life, she would die on day six. That joke stemmed from a surprise we received three months into our marriage. Michelle was pregnant.

The pregnancy wasn't necessarily a *huge* surprise. Michelle and I had been sleeping together from very early on in our relationship, and there were far too many instances when we didn't use protection. Actually, the fact that she didn't get pregnant until after we were married was a measure of God's grace.

Finding out Michelle was pregnant was a little scary but so dang exciting. I was going to be a dad. It had been three years since I'd lost that title. I was no longer hurting from the loss of Jessie, but I was still dealing with the emptiness from that wound—no longer grieving the child but instead the role of father. I was so excited to know that, beyond a shadow of a doubt, this child was mine, forever.

God, again in His kindness, was blessing me even though I wasn't yet serving Him. *Grace upon grace upon grace.*

Michelle and I both wanted kids. We had a stable environment to raise the baby in, with a supportive community of family and friends around us. We considered what it was going to take and started to prepare. We got the nursery ready, rallied everyone around us, and committed to pouring all of ourselves into that baby.

I think it's common for some guys to fixate on the idea of having a boy first. Something about wrestling with them, teaching them to play baseball, and raising a mini-me sounds so cool and manly. But that wasn't God's plan for us—we were having a girl! Funny enough, I don't even remember how we did the gender reveal, but I can tell you we didn't set a pink bomb off in our neighborhood like some to-be parents do now. Twenty-one years and two girls later, I wouldn't trade it for anything else. Being a dad to my daughters is the best, and I don't for a second think I missed out on not having a boy.

The start of our family was amazing, and so much of the way I lived changed. I took life more seriously, and worked even harder to provide a good life for them. But more responsibility brings more pressure and stress, often leading to compounded bad habits. And, my bad habits weren't going anywhere anytime soon. Though Michelle couldn't drink, smoke weed, or smoke cigarettes during her pregnancy, I could and I did. She instantly became the built-in designated driver, and I used that to my advantage.

We went to bars and parties, or had people at our house to party. Michelle was a trooper, but I know it wasn't easy for her. She later confided that the incessant party scene frustrated her, more so because she felt like I made her less of a priority than because she missed partying herself. I should have been more aware and sensitive, but I never even thought about it.

Michelle was able to join back in with the party times once our baby girl, Alexis, was born. Having a baby meant we couldn't go out much during the week anymore, but we made sure to get out every Friday or Saturday night. We occasionally drank around Alexis, but we, particularly Michelle, never overconsumed when Alexis was around. And we never used drugs around her.

Having two sets of grandparents who basically fought over watching the baby meant we were never short on babysitters. When we couldn't go out, we just brought the party home. Of our friends, we were the only ones to own a house, and we had a pool so we hosted often. Pool parties and all-night drinking games were the norm when we weren't out at the bars.

As crazy as it sounds, all of the partying never hindered my sales success at work. I was doing well, so we maintained a fun lifestyle. In retrospect, I could have made far better choices during that season of life. As a husband and father, I should have prioritized my family over partying.

THE SELFISHNESS STARTS

By 2004, three years into marriage and two years into being a daddy, I felt the need to grow professionally. I'd reached the top of the pay scale as the wholesale sales manager at Wheel Warehouse. I loved working there, but I needed to make more money.

In late 2004, I became friends with a client at Wheel Warehouse. Mike was a very cool guy who owned a wheel and tire business in south Orange County. While Mike wasn't super flashy with his money, I could tell he did well. He had a nice house in Orange County, a second home in Havasu, a bomb boat, and expensive watches. The more we hung out, the more I realized I wanted what he had. I grew up struggling for one new pair of shoes a year, and with the right job, I could buy whatever I wanted. I also wanted to provide more for Michelle and Alexis—a bigger house, nicer cars, family vacations, and toys for us all.

Mike was one of the hardest-working guys I knew. He made good money and ran a successful business, but he wasn't opposed to getting dirty, crawling underneath cars, and changing tires if that's what it took. I regularly watched him install wheels and tires on cars in the back alley of his shop.

I hit him up about the possibility of working with him to develop new business opportunities and better serve his existing clients. While it was his business, I had clients I could bring over. I also knew I could help him grow other aspects of the business, so I could be treated like a partner.

Hard work and good work ethic were important to me, ingrained in me from a young age. When I lived with my dad back in high school, I worked at his auto air-conditioning shop for about a year. Dad taught me, and at times forced me with very strong words and his heavy hand, to work hard. There was no cutting corners with my dad, whether working on a car, taking inventory, or sweeping the shop floor. Everything was done right the first time. If it wasn't, I had to own up to it and do it all over again until it was. I despised how strict my dad was with that stuff. But later, when I went to work in an environment I cared about, I was thankful. Few people worked as hard as my dad taught me to, and that gave me a serious advantage, especially when building a business.

My hard work combined with Mike's work ethic, and the opportunity to make lots more money, inspired me to negotiate a deal to go into business with Mike. The concept of working with him seemed like a no-brainer.

The first couple of months were great. I was getting familiar with how his business operated and his customers' expectations. I was bringing new clients over, too. Mike was pumped that I was there to help him, because he was busy and needed a bit of a break. A guy came in a few days a week to do installs, but for the most part, it was just me and my buddy.

I also loved the fact that I was making better money. Selling high-end wheel and tire packages to wealthy people meant we regularly exchanged thousands, if not tens of thousands, of dollars a week. Whenever we got paid in cash, that made our lives even better—my buddy was pretty fair with how he paid me, and he always kicked me a little extra from cash transactions. Some months I was making in excess of ten thousand dollars—a first for me. It was actually a big leap. In my previous job, a great month was five thousand to six thousand dollars.

As many know, earning more money usually translates to more ways to spend more money. If you'll recall, I had very little guidance in that area. My mom did her best to earn a living, but she never had to manage a lot of money. And my dad was absent, so it was up to me to determine how I spent my money. Before long, my wife was driving a nice Mercedes and I was wearing expensive watches. Such purchases weren't completely irresponsible—we could afford them—but it wasn't exactly smart spending either, considering we could have been planning better for our future.

Spending money on material items wasn't the worst. The worst was my gambling. Gambling provided a rush of adrenaline I loved and a theoretical opportunity to make more money. I had no regard for how it could negatively impact my family. Prior to befriending Mike, I had done my fair share of gambling in casinos. Blackjack and craps were my games of choice, and I enjoyed them enough to pretend like I didn't lose much money on them. But that's what every gambler says, because they rarely keep track of their losses after dusting themselves off.

Mike and a few of his friends regularly used a bookie to gamble on sports. That excited me because I didn't have to go all the way to Laughlin or Vegas to gamble. Plus, they bragged about big winnings—in fact, that's all I heard about.

It started small for me. I would bet fifty bucks on a game or three-team parlay while I watched my buddy place five hundred on the same bets. But like everything else in my life around that time—drinking, smoking cigarettes and weed, owning nice things—enough wasn't enough. I needed a little more adrenaline, a few more things, and to fit in with the crowd just a little more. I bumped to one hundred, and at times up to five hundred dollars, on some bets.

It was a crazy roller-coaster ride for a while. I would be super stressed one day, cheering out loud the next. I could be up a few hundred or down a few hundred in a week. I got pissed because we didn't have extra money and then stoked when we did. Once in a while, I would win more than one thousand dollars, which was usually back in the bookie's hand the following week. I would get mad at Michelle for spending fifteen dollars on a shirt to go out in on a Friday night but only because I'd lost $250 that week. I justified my losses with the fact that Mike was betting, and losing, even bigger, so my losses didn't feel too bad...until it all came crashing down.

The NCAA men's college basketball tourney was in full swing, and my buddy and I had just come out of an incredible run betting on professional soccer (yup, soccer). We were following this guy in an online forum that was lights out, hitting pick after pick after pick. His screen name was Mr Hotpicks, and he lived up to the name. He was picking four out of every five correctly, and we were riding his coattails. In a period of about a month, I won around five thousand dollars. It was amazing.

On that streak, we went into the NCAA tournament with tons of excitement. For those new to gambling, know that college sports are dangerous territory (actually, all gambling is dangerous and I highly advise against it). Oddsmakers determine betting lines based on proven data that tells them who will win and by how much. With pro sports, it's so dang accurate. But with college sports, especially the NCAA basketball championship, logic often flies out the window because those kids are playing with heart. That's why we see an 18-seed team beat out a 2-seed. *Heart!*

It was March Madness 2006. In the Elite Eight round, UConn was facing George Mason. While George Mason was a Cinderella story up to that point, UConn was all but guaranteed to dominate them. They'd played incredibly well all year, and all signs pointed to that continuing.

So, we rode it, and big. I don't remember exactly how much I had on that game, but it was either going to create a windfall of cash or put me in the worst hole I'd ever been in—maxed out credit cards and possibly even a missed mortgage payment. Michelle wouldn't have known since she chose not to be involved in our finances, but I would have been so stressed that she definitely would have sensed something was seriously wrong. I was on edge the whole game, and then into overtime, UConn, the favorite, lost by two points. That brought my losses for that week to five grand.

I called Mike immediately after the game. I was angry and defeated, not only because I lost all that money but also because I let myself get there. I felt so stupid for letting influences, like Mike and his buddies, who had far more money than I did, get the best of me. Mike tried to talk me off the ledge, telling me it was just a bad week and that I would get it back. That wasn't going to happen, because it never does in the long run. Regardless, that isn't why I was so broken.

I was broken because Michelle didn't know how bad my habit had gotten. I hadn't offered her any info about my sports gambling, and she didn't pay attention to our finances. I knew that and took advantage of it. While keeping secrets from her, though, I was risking our money the whole time. A good husband would, um, never have gambled like that.

An even better husband is open and upfront with his wife at all times, even on the heels of his missteps. I hadn't been honest, and my excuse to myself was that she never asked and therefore didn't need to know. If I had told her from the beginning, she could have weighed in on my gambling decisions and maybe prevented some bad ones. And even if I had still made poor choices, she likely would have been right there to pick me up when I fell. Instead, I lied to Michelle about it all.

Michelle saw how rattled I was and wanted to know why.

"What's wrong, baby?" she asked.

"I lost a lot of money gambling," I replied, "on a bunch of games this week."

"Well, how much?" she asked. She wanted to comfort and support me.

And yet I continued to deceive her. "About a thousand dollars," I lied.

"It's OK, baby. That is a lot, but we will figure it out." She hugged me.

I felt like an asshole, a total loser—not just because I lost the money but for lying to the person who most loved me.

Getting caught up in the money wasn't the only challenge working with my buddy. Shortly after we began our business partnership, Mike unfortunately separated from his wife and would later divorce her. That was hard for a few reasons. For one, Michelle and I were good friends with him and his wife. We spent quite a bit of time together. Second, divorce is stress-inducing, and he was stressed. He was having a bit of a hard time focusing, since he was regularly meeting with lawyers and had a load on his mind.

Last, he suddenly was free to do whatever he wanted. This became bad news for me and my marriage.

SELFISHNESS COLLIDES WITH SEX

Marriage was an amazing gift that made me so happy and fulfilled, but it was unrealistic to expect Michelle to heal my past wounds. Without healing from my past, my marriage was a temporary bandage—and it was beginning to bleed through to reveal the sexual wound that had been there all along.

Mike was going out quite a bit, and from time to time, I joined him—Lakers and Angels games, bars and clubs, and even strip joints. Of course, my getting caught up in that wasn't his fault but mine. And that season of life accelerated the destructive path I was on.

Going out with Mike didn't feel like a big deal—just boys being boys. I had so much fun being out with him, living the lavish life of bottle service and front row seats. Being honest with Michelle about where I was going was a big challenge, and I often failed. I never told her I was going to strip clubs, and she never asked. None of that mattered, because I was lying to cover up my wrongdoings.

Some married men justify that going to a strip club is OK if they "don't do anything." But staring at a naked woman who isn't your wife breaks the marriage covenant, and I did that. I am ashamed to admit that I also went beyond that. I never had skin-to-skin contact, but I sometimes went way over the line by getting lap dances. I am disgusted with myself for that. Back then, I wasn't too hard on myself about those feelings. Even if I felt regret the next morning, I didn't let it get to me too much. But reflecting now on those moments, I am still sick about what I did.

I was spiraling, and it took its toll on Michelle and me. My biggest challenges were the distractions from focusing attention on my marriage and spending money I didn't really have. Arguments ensued between us, typically around money. If she bought something unnecessary, but inexpensive, I got on her about it. She often fired back about something I did that she didn't like or didn't do that she wanted me to. The arguments escalated, getting louder and more intense.

We were both frustrated. Michelle later shared that even though she was putting in so much effort for our family, I didn't give her any credit for the work she did at home nor did I help her much with household responsibilities. At the time, I felt justified since I was working and earning the money. In reality, I was a selfish man who wanted what I wanted, doing less to provide for and protect the woman to whom I was eternally committed.

We still had plenty of good days, going out together and having fun. We had loving sex semi-regularly. But the tension was building, and it was about to blow and turn very ugly. Thankfully, we used words and never got physically aggressive, but it was still bad and I am ashamed of it.

Then, during a particularly heated argument, likely about money issues and my shortcomings around family obligations, I screamed, "If we can't get along, maybe we should just get a divorce!"

Michelle seemed surprised, but out of anger, she yelled, "Maybe we should!"

I guess divorce seemed like the easy way out, but it wasn't. We had a four-year-old, and after growing up with a weekend father, I did not want that for my child. But what were the alternatives? I felt justified in my anger due to what I perceived as her frivolous spending, her not listening to me when I wanted something done a certain way, and her lack of fulfilling my unrealistic expectations. I was driving my wife away. I was turning into the man who had hurt me so badly—my dad. I never intended to repeat history when I got married, but I was wounded. In turn, I was wounding Michelle. Silence between us became the norm.

Then, I got a taste of the consequences of repeatedly abandoning and hurting my wife.

I have no idea why I logged in to Michelle's email that morning, but I did. I found a conversation she had with another guy. Its context wasn't particularly inappropriate, but it was personal enough that it stung. I kept digging and found she had sent him a photo of her in a Halloween costume. She looked so pretty, and it killed me that she had sent it to him.

I didn't know what to do or how to handle it, but my hurt turned to anger. I went into the office that morning and told Mike what I had found. I showed him the conversations, and his immediate reaction was that I had to confront Michelle. Though he was experiencing his own marital challenges, he wasn't influencing me to leave. He really liked and respected Michelle, but he knew I couldn't let this go. I couldn't let it fester.

I called Michelle at work and told her I needed to talk to her, that it was an emergency and couldn't wait. I needed to meet her as soon as she could step out of the office. She nervously agreed, and I headed over there.

I drove to her office, shaking the whole time—all the anger, hurt, and worry over what I might find out. Michelle wasn't the cheating type, so that wasn't a valid possibility. But I was thinking irrationally, and irrational thoughts become possibilities.

I pulled into the parking lot, and Michelle got into my truck. "Hey, what's up?" she asked.

I looked into her eyes and asked, "Do you have anything to tell me?"

"Tell you, like, what?" She was confused.

"Is there anything that you need to tell me?" I asked again, this time with a bit of anger in my voice.

"No," she said emphatically. I had printed out the online conversation, and I threw the papers at her. "What? What is this?" she asked.

"Look! Look at it!" I yelled.

She said, "I met him in an online poker room."

"Who is he? Why did you email him?" I asked.

"He lives in another country, and it's nothing. We are just friends, nothing more."

"Is that it? Is there anything more than this?" I pressed her.

"No, that is it—just friendly conversation."

"Have you ever talked to him outside of email?"

"No, just email, I swear."

Who could blame her for talking to someone else? I wasn't always the easiest to talk to, and we had been arguing so much. Still, I was pissed. Nothing much was resolved, but we each had said our part before we both returned to work.

I couldn't let the situation go. Something didn't sit right with me, so I dug deeper. I looked at our cell phone bills and found out the two had talked by phone on a few occasions. She told me they had never spoken, and that was a lie, which sent me over the edge. I wasn't sure if I wanted to fight for my marriage or just check out.

Even worse, Michelle wasn't the only one dipping a toe outside of the marriage. I wasn't talking to one particular woman, but I flirted with other women when I was in bars without my wife. I was also frequenting strip clubs, checking out naked women and getting lap dances. Who the hell was I to say anything?

One might expect that to have cleared my head out a little bit, but it didn't. I hadn't considered that I was in large part to blame for what happened. I wasn't present for my wife. I wasn't listening to her or supporting her. I was working my ass off to provide for my family and reasoned that it was enough. The truth is that working my ass off was far from what my family needed. They needed a husband and father to love them unconditionally, to serve them in their needs, to sacrifice his needs for theirs, and to make sure they knew they were always his first priority. I was not ready to be the man they needed me to be.

APPLYING THE WOUND-ANALYSIS FRAMEWORK

Having sex far too young, and irresponsibly, distorted my view of healthy relationships in general, and sexual relationships more specifically. That sent a ripple through my dating life and right into my marriage. I quickly lost sight of my responsibility to the woman I loved most, getting caught up with a friend who had abandoned his marriage. As a result, I risked walking the road to destruction of my marriage.

Reflecting back on, and working through, the Wound of Selfishness and Sex has given me a clearer view of myself and helped me consistently walk the path to which God has called me.

Acknowledge the hurt.

The self-inflicted wound of sex was the result of having sex at a very young and outside the marriage covenant. Meanwhile, the self-inflicted wound of selfishness was the result of posturing, not listening, and being a poor leader. Both parts of this wound led me down the darkest path of my life.

Realize the effect.

The Wound of Selfishness and Sex affected my life in three major ways:

1. I wasn't present for my family when they most needed me. Leaving a lot of the day-to-day home and family tasks to my wife, I missed some very important moments of my oldest daughter's childhood. I worked long hours, justifying my absence from the home by convincing myself I was giving them a better life by making money. In reality, I was working to support my gambling and partying so I could fit in with others who were more affluent.

2. In part because my self-confidence was eroding, I was caught up trying to be someone I wasn't. My gambling cost my family tens of thousands of dollars. My "go big or go home" approach didn't play well in that arena. Little by little, I was lost.

3. Having sex so young meant carrying all that sexual baggage into my relationship with my wife. My words and actions pushed my wife away, leading her to not want to talk to me about life and instead talk to another man. That was a serious blow to my self-confidence and to our marriage.

Unlock the greatness.

God used the Wound of Selfishness and Sex to show me the world doesn't revolve around me.

I wouldn't say I was completely self-centered, but as I found professional success and got noticed as a good-looking guy—leading to what could have easily become more sexual opportunities—it definitely got to my head.

After a few more months of marital struggles, I found God—and He revealed to me my shortcomings. In the next chapter, I share more about the final tipping point that forced me to seek God, in the next chapter. For now, I will say this. I had to know God, as well as who He created me to be and what He had planned for my life, before I could even begin to heal from this wound. I would never have been able to figure that out on my own.

As I eventually studied the Bible, sat with other faithful Christian men, and repented of my sin, God revealed to me the gifts and talents He has given me. I refocused, moving from a me-focused life to a God-focused one. I saw that God gave me gifts, and equipped me in certain ways, for the good of myself and others. This shift in mindset has helped me make a far greater impact in this world. I believe that as I continue to mature, God will use me for even greater purposes.

Before any such greatness could be realized, I needed to see how dark my heart could be. I desperately needed God to rescue me.

5

WOUNDED BY BROKENNESS

IT WAS APRIL 2006, AND MY BUDDY MIKE AND I WEREN'T working out as a business team. He had too much going on, and I was trying to pick up the pace. The added stress wasn't helpful for my marriage, which at that point was kind of just existing as Michelle and I weaved through good days and bad days. I wasn't around much for my daughter, who was four years old at the time, because I was trying to pick up the slack Mike had left. I needed a job change, to better myself professionally but also to get my marriage and family into a better spot.

It was time to move on. My stepdad, Tom, worked for Orange County Blueprint (OCB), an amazing family-owned business in SoCal. OCB was a document management and print company that provided blueprint and graphics printing services to the construction industry. The company was riding the amazing wave of the booming housing market, and I wanted to be part of it. I knew I could make a lot of money as a sales rep. It was a very good opportunity, and I wanted to make it work.

But there was a big problem. Tom did not want to hire me. He was a man of utmost integrity and was reluctant to insert nepotism into the company dynamic. A little part of me also suspects he didn't want to risk putting me in the position because after witnessing my life over the last few years, he wasn't completely confident I had my crap together. I get it.

Tom refused to even interview me for the position. He wasn't mean or rude, but being a cocky twenty-eight-year-old with a successful sales record, I wasn't taking no for an answer, regardless of Tom's reasons. I told Tom I would go over his head. If he wasn't going to hire me, I would call the CEO and tell him Tom was costing the company money by not hiring me. It sounds ridiculous, but I said it. Tom held to his word...and so did I. I requested a meeting with the CEO, and he obliged.

This was the first real interview I had ever had. All my previous job opportunities were referral-based. This interview required slacks, a dress shirt, a tie, and a jacket. Though Tom didn't want to show nepotism, he wanted me to succeed. He knew my work ethic and talent combined with OCB's track record would add up to success. So, he helped me pick out the appropriate attire and prepped with me. Tom was, as usual, being the best dad he could be.

On the day of the interview, I showed up ready to go. (I'd also ditched the tongue piercing and the earrings.) I gave the CEO every bit of me and committed to crushing it for him and the company. He hired me on the spot, offered to pay me more than I had ever made before, and even gave me a signing bonus.

I wish I could say I knew it would happen that way, but at best I had only hoped. In hindsight, hope had little to do with it. Talent and skill didn't play in either. God did. He put me into that position because my marriage was on the rocks, and this job—and some unexpected choices I would make there—could be the rescue mission my marriage needed.

THE LOWEST POINT I'D EVER HIT

After a few months of training, getting to know my colleagues, and learning the client base, I was set to go to Chicago for a few days of sales training. I was pumped because I had never been to Chicago. I was looking forward to the food, drinks, sights—and the potential opportunity to cheat on my wife.

I am absolutely disgusted and ashamed to admit that, but it's true. I was in a bad way—wounded by my sin, hurt by my wife's relationship with the other guy, and so twisted up that I struggled to know what was right anymore. I didn't have a woman friend there, or even in mind. I just knew I would be far away from home and the people who knew me well. Cheating was my next step in the trajectory I was on. I'd flirted with other women, so in the right setting with a willing participant, cheating seemed inevitable.

I traveled with a colleague, Darren. A leader in the company, he was facilitating some of the training in Chicago. Because my stepdad had worked for OCB for many years, I'd attended many company events and had previously met Darren. When I started at OCB, he was one of the first leaders I attached myself to. He was a great guy with wonderful values and, unbeknownst to me, a man God brought into my life to stand alongside me in my greatest time of need.

We landed in Chicago late on a Sunday evening and settled into our hotel for the night. The following morning, we headed into our first day of training. Our company was transitioning from regional private firm to national public company, so the training was comprised of men and women from all around the country. We met and chatted throughout the day, and we were challenged to become better salespeople. A few of us bonded and hung out in the evenings.

On the final night, a group of us went out to explore the city. We hit up the Hancock building for the view and then had drinks in some cool local bars. We all ended up back at the hotel bar and kept the party going into the wee hours of the morning.

I was flirting with one woman in particular. There was nothing unique about her—just a woman who was there in my very weak moment. She laughed at my jokes, participated in conversations whatever the topic, and gave me the attention I felt I deserved. Because I thought I was somehow being shortchanged at home, any extra attention stroked my ego.

Sure, I thought about my wife and daughter at home. But I didn't think about how my actions could be so disrespectful and destructive to my family. I was thinking of ways to navigate what might happen should I engage sexually with that woman. I kept drinking to numb my conscience.

Then came the moment that had the potential to change my entire life. The woman asked, "My room or yours?"

My mind raced. *Is this really going to happen?*

On the flight to Chicago, I considered a moment like this. But I hadn't rehearsed a conversation, so I never thought about turning down the opportunity...until I did. As much as the idea of sex with another woman had seemed appealing in my mind, I couldn't do it. I couldn't cross that line because of what it would have done to my wife, my daughter, and myself.

"Good night," I said to the woman. I rode the elevator up to my room, alone. That decision deterred what surely would have been a life-altering act. Although I didn't give God credit at the time, He protected me from potentially sleeping with that woman and ruining everything I now know as good. I believe that God, by the power of his Spirit at work in me, caused me to ponder the consequences.

The next morning, preparing to head home, I was in utter disbelief about what almost happened and the life position I was in. I had practically everything I ever wanted—a beautiful wife, an adorable daughter, a nice house in a prominent SoCal zip code, a Mercedes, and a great-paying job with so much potential. Friends looked up to me, and others envied me.

I realized how broken I was. I was a hollow shell of a man, empty and unfulfilled by all I thought I needed to fulfill me. I had tried everything to be happy, like making good money and owning nice stuff. At times, to fix my marriage, I worked on my communication and tried for a few days here and there to focus all my attention on Michelle. Nothing was working.

My mom had sacrificed her whole life for me, but I was no longer a son to be proud of. My dad left me when I needed him most, and yet I'd left my family too. I felt so full of shame for the man I had become. All the material success I had achieved seemed worthless, and the only thing that mattered—my family life—was an utter failure. But in my own power to fix my life, I had run out of options.

The only option I had left was to consider God. My Catholic upbringing, and the prodding of friends over the years, reminded me a loving God was out there. This led me to the biggest question I'd ever asked: "Should give God a shot?"

AN UNEXPECTED TURNING POINT

When Darren and I got to the airport, we learned some sort of terrorist activity had occurred at another airport, so O'Hare was in a major holding pattern. Our flight was delayed quite a few hours, so we headed to an airport restaurant to grab a bite and sit out the delay. We both ordered some food, but Darren also ordered a blue cocktail. I was blown away because I knew Darren was a Christian.

"Dude, how in the heck can you order a cocktail?" I asked. "I thought you were a Christian." Darren was always very open about his Christianity but in a non-confrontational way.

Laughing, Darren replied, "Christians can drink. They just need to do so responsibly."

"That's crazy. I never knew that. I thought you guys couldn't have any fun," I said, only half-joking.

Darren chuckled and shut down my ignorance with a quick lesson in responsible drinking. He could surely smell my hangover, so this was one of many lessons I needed to learn.

"I grew up Catholic, and have a lot of issues with the religion and what I saw in the church. Can you tell me a little bit more about Christianity and what it means to you?" I asked.

Darren didn't get to fully answer my question before we were called to board our plane. We were seated next to each other on the five-plus hour flight, so I asked a few more questions about his faith. I shared what had been going on the last few years of my life, particularly in my marriage. I also confessed what had nearly happened the night before.

Instead of jumping down my throat for being a complete idiot over the years and a near disaster the previous night, Darren shared kindly and openly about Christianity. That conversation made me realize I would never be happy living my life as I had been.

A good friend and neighbor, Dean, was also in my ear pretty regularly about Christianity. He and his wife, Tracy (not to be confused with framily member Tracy mentioned earlier in my story), attended a local Calvary Chapel. Dean had been inviting me for years, but I was having none of it...until I was out of options and decided to give God a shot.

I got home and told Michelle that I was ready to go to church. I didn't have to give her a reason. It would be years before I explained to her what happened at the hotel. I was too ashamed, scared to further wreck our marriage, and ill-equipped to handle any instant repercussions. We'd talked before about going to church. We'd both grown up going to church, and having some sense of it still inside of us, we often talked about attending after Alexis was born. We wanted her to be brought up with a good values-based foundation. A lot of people do that, right? They go to church to gain, or maintain, some semblance of morality. But on top of that, Michelle was also ready to do whatever it took to fix our marriage and apparently felt finding God was the way to do it.

What a joke that was to think improving my morality, just going to church, would actually work. I didn't need morality—I needed a complete transformation.

COMING TO FAITH

The following Sunday, Michelle and I committed to joining Dean and Tracy at church. After hearing so many stories about their amazing senior pastor, and how great the church was overall, we had to check it out. Dean and Tracy unfortunately couldn't make it to church that week. Without the comfort of friends to walk in with us, that could have been a deal-breaker. But we went anyway. We knew we needed it.

Michelle and I walked into that Calvary Chapel in August 2006, and life was never again the same. The church was big, with worshipers filling approximately eight hundred seats. Being familiar with church from my upbringing, I didn't feel it was necessarily foreign. But it felt overwhelming and lonely. I had a feeling everyone knew I didn't fit in and that my life was a huge mess. Guilt had a way of making me think crazy thoughts. Though Michelle and I had talked about taking Alexis to church, we left her with my parents that Sunday.

We were looking forward to hearing that amazing senior pastor preach, but he wasn't there. Instead, an assistant pastor stood in for him. I felt momentarily let down, deflated. I thought I needed something big and that the main guy was the only one who could bring it.

But all I needed was someone to faithfully share from the Word of God, and that's exactly what I got. The assistant pastor opened his Bible and preached. Interestingly, I don't remember the verses he read or most of what he said. But clearly his main points were to encourage men to be godly husbands and fathers.

Then that I saw it—God had intentionally brought me to that low place in my life. While the idea of God's sovereignty and man's free will has been debated for eternity, to me, it is clear. God is in control of all things. He had orchestrated every moment, good and bad. The good was initiated and fulfilled by God; the bad was initiated by the sinfulness of humans (me and others) but used by God to bring about His good. Every single event in my life was deliberately leading up to that day. For so long, I tried to figure out and fulfill my life's purpose, but God had created me for His specific purpose—He formed all of my days for me, even before I was born (Psalm 139:13–16).

God had lovingly held a mirror up to me for years, showing me how broken I was—not to shame me but to save me. While I had done a lot of good, I wasn't good enough. I would never be good enough. I would never on my own be a righteous husband, father, or man. I needed Jesus Christ to save me from myself and lead me into the fullness of who God had created me to be.

The other eight hundred people in church that morning got a great sermon, but I got a changed life—well, at least the beginnings of one. "That was such a great sermon. It was exactly what I needed to hear. We definitely need to make this a regular part of our life now," I said to Michelle. She agreed.

Michelle and I knew we needed to attend church, and seek faith, on a more consistent basis. We needed to recognize God as the center point of our life, our marriage, and our family.

It was heartfelt and well-intentioned, but real change proved to be a lot more challenging.

FINAL WAKE-UP CALL

For the next six months, our spiritual progress happened in fits and starts. We attended church nearly every Sunday. Often though, I was still hungover from Saturday. As the offering plate got passed around, I dropped the same amount of money into the offering plate as I had dropped in the bar the night before. A bit of my old Catholic guilt had come back to haunt me. It didn't help that we weren't consistently connecting with other Christians. That was the byproduct of being new to a large church and taking no initiative to get involved. But it also didn't help that while people were kind on Sundays, none dug any deeper to get to know us. We weren't invited to participate in any activities beyond the Sunday gathering.

My final wakeup call happened on St. Patrick's Day 2007. As most people know, St. Patty's Day is a great excuse to party...hard. My best friend, Chad (yes, Chad from Route 91) and I went to The Slidebar in downtown Fullerton around lunchtime for food and a few drinks. I'd called a few other friends to join us.

Throughout the early part of the day, I communicated back and forth with Michelle. She knew where I was, whom I was with, and what I was doing. I told her I would be home no later than dinnertime. But more friends showed up. They kept showing up. The bar's entrance was a turnstile of friends who wanted to join the party. At one point, twenty people must have squeezed around our table, mostly drinking beer but with an occasional shot.

Two hours turned to four, four to six, and before I knew it—I really *didn't* know it because I was too drunk—it was dinnertime, and Michelle wanted to know where the heck I was. My phone rang, and I picked up. "Yo, what's up?" I said.

"Where are you?" Michelle was pissed.

"We're hanging out. What's wrong with you?" I knew exactly what was wrong.

"Get home," she demanded.

Click. I hung up on her.

Finally, sometime around 9:00 p.m., I drove home, so drunk and so stupid. Greeted by an angry wife, I decided to go to battle. "Why are you so pissed? Just relax," I said to her.

"Relax? Relax! You said you were going to be home hours ago, and instead, you show up at the end of the night, hammered. What is wrong with you?"

The argument did not end well for me, and Michelle was beyond angry. Maybe even more deep than anger though was her disappointment. Six months earlier we had made a commitment to each other to change, do better, and leave the irresponsible and selfish behavior behind. In a few hours, I had blown up that commitment and let my wife down.

The next morning, I woke up with enough memory to know I was a complete idiot. I was an idiot for drinking so much, drinking all day, driving home drunk, lying to Michelle about when I would be home, arguing with her, and letting myself, my marriage, and my life get back to the dark valley I'd lived in for so long. That was it, and I knew it. I couldn't continue to live my life that way. I needed to be all in on Jesus or not in on Jesus at all. With Him, my life and marriage would be victorious. Without Him, I would be divorced and maybe even dead.

I chose Jesus.

DOING THE WORK TO GROW MY FAITH—FINALLY

Michelle and I started figuring out what cultivating our faith meant. We raised our hands and got involved at church so we could meet other people, learn from them, and even have some of them hold us accountable to the life we wanted to live. We talked to people before and after church on Sundays. And to learn more about Jesus, we signed up for extracurricular classes outside of the Sunday church service.

I was making progress in baby steps, and it felt nice. But there was something else I felt I needed to do. I felt deeply convicted that I needed to drastically change my surroundings. I slowly withdrew from my longtime group of friends. It was one of the hardest decisions I have ever made. I had grown up with some of the guys, including Chad and Casey. We had played baseball and ridden bikes on our block. We went to school together. Some were in my wedding, and we loved one another so damn much.

Look, I know every mistake I've made in my life was my own doing. These guys never made me do anything. As a matter of fact, I was one of the worst hooligans of them all. That said, some influences were too strong for me to resist. Against Michelle's pleading, I completely pulled away to hang around only with other Christians. I felt it had to be done for that season of my life. I have since reconnected with most of those old friends—yes, Chad and Casey included—and have the most amazing, close friendships with them. I love them with all my heart and can't imagine my life now without them.

But back then, the support of my Christian friends gave me the best chance to stay grounded in Jesus—because they grounded their lives and marriages in Jesus. When I sought the truth, they pointed me to Jesus. If I fell short, they loved me like Jesus does. They reminded me that apart from Jesus I can do nothing at all (John 15:5). I felt safe being myself with them, because those of us inside the church know we are messed up.

Great English preacher Charles Spurgeon once said, "If I had never joined a church till I had found one that was perfect, I should never have joined one at all. And the moment I did join it, if I had found one, I should have spoiled it, for it would not have been a perfect church after I had become a member of it. Still, imperfect as it is, it is the dearest place on earth to us." In the church, with the church, was where I needed to be.

The next few years were challenging but equally fruitful. Challenging because I was constantly fighting to kill the sin that had entangled me for so long. Fruitful because I desired to serve God and His people by going on a mission trip to Haiti—and eventually planting and pastoring a church in Orange County. Those roles gave me a greater sense of purpose and filled my soul, enabling me to pour so much more love and joy into my family.

Michelle and I continued to work on our marriage, joining a Bible group for young married couples. The group was led by the assistant pastor who had preached the message on our first day in the church. We were learning how to fulfill our biblical roles as husband and wife. I was also learning more about what it means to be a father.

I felt the changes happening inside of me. I began to understand the implications of verses like Ephesians 5:25 in which the Apostle Paul says, "Husbands, love your wives, as Christ loved the church and gave himself up for her." I realized Jesus Christ, the Son of God, came down to this earth to literally die for me. He gave up every bit of himself on the cross for me. And somehow, someway, Paul says I am to act similarly for my wife. Sure, there might come a day when I actually have to sacrifice my life for hers—I would be challenged to that at a later date in our marriage during the Route 91 shooting—but it doesn't mean only that. It also means I am to sacrifice my wants, needs, time, money, hopes, and dreams, for my wife. If needing to give up my life for my wife is the extreme sacrifice in Paul's call to men, every lesser form of sacrifice is appropriate. I wanted to do that. I wanted to be that man.

You see, my love for Michelle never ceased. She was my best friend before we got married, and I loved her deeply from the moment we said, "I do." But I didn't know the depth of Christ-centered love. I didn't fully understand "for better or worse, in sickness and in health" when I vowed them on our wedding day. This type of covenant love could be revealed only once I saw God was revealing Himself to me. That part of my heart, mind, and soul had yet to be unlocked. My self-sustenance needed to be broken down. The walls I had put up need to be torn down. The false idols I erected needed to be destroyed. It was going to hurt. No matter the source of my wounds, I needed to acknowledge and experience them if I was to be built all the way back up.

As I loved Michelle more, through service and sacrifice, she loved me more. The more she loved me, through service and sacrifice, the more I loved her. It was a beautiful circle.

The year 2009 brought us an exciting gift. God blessed us with another child, daughter number two. Alexis was seven, and we'd recently celebrated our eighth wedding anniversary. I had thought I was perfectly content with one daughter, but God knew better. While our daughter Chloe was just as much of a surprise as Alexis had been, God had been preparing us for her arrival. Chloe brought even more life and joy into our family, which was already thriving.

COMMITMENT BECOMES COVENANT

Covenants in the Bible are unbreakable promises God makes to His people. After consistently attending church for five years, and spending time in close fellowship with other worshipers, Michelle and I gained a much better understanding of what the Bible says about marriage—primarily, that it is more than a commitment. It is a covenant, an unbreakable promise made between a man and a woman. The promise is to love, comfort, honor, and keep each other, in sickness and in health, and, forsaking all others, be faithful to each other as long as they both live.

As our ten-year wedding anniversary neared, Michelle and I wanted to make something big of it. Five years prior, we were on the road to divorce. At times, we only existed in the same space instead of living as a one-flesh union. By the grace of God, we'd overcome so much and were in a great place. We were madly in love, and our family of four was thriving. We wanted to celebrate that and stamp it into our story. The best way we knew to do that was to go before the Lord, witnessed by our family and closest friends, and restate our vows as the covenant God intended it to be. We approached our pastor with the idea, and he was in full agreement.

We set the date—March 19, 2011. We invited family and friends to witness the work God had done in our lives. God's work had transformed me from a selfish man into a servant-hearted one. I was done setting unrealistic expectations of my wife. I would no longer put her or our family through any harm for something I did or said. God had shown me Michelle's beauty, both inner and outer, and I couldn't wait to share that with all in attendance.

As I said the words, "For better or worse, in sickness and in health, from this day forward, until death do us part," this time I finally knew what they would require of me, and I had never been more certain of anything in my life. "I do!" I declared with all of the confidence in the world. Those vows meant more to me than they had ten years prior. I understood how God created marriage, and formed man and woman to be in partnership. I felt the weight of every single word.

I stared into Michelle's eyes, and for one final time, I said, "I am sorry for all the ways I came up short, all the ways in which I was not the husband you deserved nor needed me to be. I love you more than I ever have, and I cannot wait to spend the rest of our lives together." I needed to repent to Michelle, before our family and friends. I also made a covenant to Michelle that I would do everything in my power to honor, love, serve, sacrifice for, provide for, and protect her. I cried joyfully as the pastor said, "What God has joined together, man cannot separate."

That was the final seal of confidence that Michelle and I would never again be separated physically, mentally, emotionally, or spiritually.

CHANGES KEEP COMING

My newfound faith affected not only my marriage but also my job and social habits. I applied my faith to the ways I sold to and served my clients at Orange County Blueprint, as well as how I acted at work. My words came with a new sense of truth and care for how I could help clients.

Prior to becoming a Christian, I usually tried to do the right thing for my employers or my clients, but every so often I put myself first with no regard as to how it negatively impacted others. I was fortunate to be a very good salesperson, and as such, I put up very good numbers for OCB. Putting up good numbers allowed me to goof off on the regular. As long as my numbers were good, I went into work late or cut out early to play a round of golf with a buddy. But after becoming a Christian, I found it much harder, and eventually, impossible to do that. I felt like I was stealing from the company by not giving it my all every day.

When dealing with my clients, I no longer made excuses for why someone on my sales team dropped the ball or why I forgot to follow through on something. I immediately owned up to mistakes.

While it felt good to reject dishonesty, it badly burned me one time. I had landed an incredible client—one of the largest contractors in the country. After two years of being pursued, they finally gave me (and the company) a shot. The buyer was a no-BS woman, and I was warned from day one that a slipup would do us in. Well, we slipped up. And I had an opportunity to cover it up with a lie. My boss wanted me to lie, knowing it was our best shot at keeping the client. I couldn't do it. I called the client and told her the whole truth. She appreciated my honesty, but she had made it clear—one mistake and we were done. And...we were done.

The company lost a ton of revenue, and I lost significant commission. But I felt at peace with losing because I had done the right thing. It was such a mind-blowing transformation, because a few years prior, I would have lied my way right out of that situation since losing was not an option for me.

Meanwhile, in the business world, "harmless" flirting happens all the time, as do shady relationships even between married coworkers or associates. But flirting is not harmless when people are in committed relationships, So I handled my relationships with female colleagues and clients differently. I didn't cut them off, but

I made sure not to engage in inappropriate conversations and to never put myself in positions in which we were completely alone together. Again, I was doing my best to prevent the wrong influences, whether real or perceived.

My final big change during that time was related to alcohol. After the incident with Michelle on St. Patrick's Day 2007, I'd done a better job of managing my alcohol intake. I would still partake in a few beers or a whiskey every now and again, but I wasn't getting drunk and never let it have control over me. Michelle and I drank socially from time to time, either out for dinner or around the pool on weekends. But God, by way of my oldest daughter Alexis, showed me I needed further change.

We were preparing to host a pool party at our house for members of our Bible study group. Michelle and I were getting everything cleaned up and ready when Alexis, who was around nine, said, "Daddy, do you want me to get everyone beers when they come over for the party?" Her words floored me. I realized I had conditioned my young daughter to associate all parties with alcohol and, worse, to believe she was the beer runner. Some might call that cute, but I saw it as desensitizing my child to the negative aspects of alcohol.

Those words from Alexis also made me consider the value alcohol added to my life. And to be honest, it was of no value at all. I didn't need to drink to fit in or have fun. I decided to stop drinking completely. For me, moderation wouldn't cut it. I had to wipe it clean so alcohol consumption no longer had control over me. I didn't even make a big deal about it at first—I simply cut it out and felt that if I was to ever enjoy alcohol again, I would just know.

I had no time line in mind, and five years later, I exchanged in a very helpful and powerful conversation with a fellow pastor. He encouraged me to see that I could responsibly drink while still honoring God. After much prayer, I took his advice and am now enjoying an occasional bourbon or glass of wine without jeopardizing who I want to be as a man.

This process was less about the alcohol and more about my healing brokenness by taking back control of the man God made me to be.

APPLYING THE WOUND-ANALYSIS FRAMEWORK

It's hard to admit I couldn't see how broken I was back in 2006. Without my life coming to the brink of disaster by way of a shameful interaction with another woman, I would never have seen the beauty of God and the amazing marriage, and life, he had planned for me all along.

Acknowledge the hurt.

My self-inflicted wound of brokenness, happening multiple times during this season, resulted from my unrealistic expectations of and poor communication with my wife. These led to harsh arguments and hurtful words, and my complete selfishness had me believing I took no fault in our marital issues. I felt I had liberty to do anything, and talk to anyone, I wanted to. It was like death by a thousand cuts.

Realize the effect.

Allowing myself to become broken affected my life in two major ways:

1. I nearly lost my marriage, the most important relationship in my life. I was scared at the thought of losing my wife, hurt that she felt disconnected from me, and unsure there was any way to make it right.

2. I was forced into a state of darkness and fear. All but lost, I had no idea how to fix myself. I had tried everything on my own, but I was only making my life worse, as well as the lives of those I loved.

Unlock the greatness.

Recognizing the Wound of Brokenness strengthened me in two major ways:

1. God used the Wound of Brokenness to repair my marriage. Nearly losing my wife made me realize how much I loved her. At my lowest point, I could think only of her and the life we desired to have together the day we said, "I do." I wanted that life and was willing to do anything to make it happen.

2. God used the wound of brokenness to bring me to faith in Jesus Christ. Coming to faith in Christ opened my heart and my mind to a whole new life of possibilities. My brokenness provided the path to reconciliation with God for all the bad I had done, with my wife after the mess I'd made of my marriage, and eventually, with my dad to loosen the wedge between us. A relationship with God gave me a new perspective on life and how to live it. God became my source of strength and comfort. He empowered me to take healthy risks and say no to future temptations.

I believe with my whole heart that apart from Christ, greatness is impossible. But with Him, possibilities are limitless. I would soon need the assurance of Christ's limitless strength, as mine was about to be tested again through a series of professional trials.

6

WOUNDED BY FAILURE

WHILE THE FIRST TEST OF MY FAITH WAS TO REBUILD MY marriage, which by the grace of God was doing quite well, I was about to be tested many more times in ways I didn't see coming.

There is a misconception that Christianity frees us from hardship. Some irresponsible pastors and evangelists compel people to come to Christ with promises of a better life. When the Bible is foreign to us, we can only understand a better life as defined by the world—less problems, more money, and unceasing happiness. But that is not what Christianity promises. Jesus tells His disciples that in this world they will have tribulation (John 16:33). The good news for me was that I understood and accepted that.

The bad news was that I wasn't prepared to deal with the tribulations. I thought my newfound faith, coupled with a refocused desire to do right in the world, was all I needed to overcome anything thrown my way. But God was preparing to show me that it wasn't always my strength that would get me through tough times, but it was my weakness. For in my weakness, God is my strength (2 Corinthians 12:9).

FORCED OUT OF MY COMFORTABLE JOB

By early 2007, I was crushing it for American Reprographics Company (ARC), which was the same company previously known as OCB. While I had been successful previous to my faith conversion, winning many awards and regularly recognized for my new business production, my spiritual transformation opened the door for me to be taken more seriously by leadership, peers, and notable clients. I gained those opportunities not for the mere fact that I was a Christian, but because Christianity guided me to consider others before myself, serve others as often as I could, and to carry myself in a more respectable manner.

The company's executive leadership took note of my transformation, which positively affected my performance, promoting me in 2008 to regional sales manager. In late 2009, I was nominated to participate in a global leadership program created to groom future leaders to run ARC divisions elsewhere in the country. I was recognized by high-level executives at some of the largest companies in our industry, and this opened the door for me to be chosen to serve on the Board of Directors for the Building Industry Association of Southern California, Riverside County Chapter. I was the youngest member ever to serve on the board.

While there was much to be pumped about, like everyone else we were trying to navigate the effects of the 2008 recession. It had hit us pretty hard because our business was directly tied to the building industry, with the large majority of our revenue coming from new residential construction, which was in a slump. Making it more difficult was the fact that by that time, ours was a publicly traded company. That meant we were responsible not only to ourselves but also shareholders who owned company stock.

As revenue fell, we fought to reduce costs and diversify revenue streams in hopes of lessening the blow. During the 2010 calendar year, our division of more than seven hundred employees was cut back to just over two hundred. I was sad to see friends lose their jobs, but thankfully, I was still finding new opportunities whenever they popped up. That made me feel damn good and pretty untouchable...until I wasn't.

In April 2011, my boss, Bob, who had only recently beat me for the position of vice president of sales, called me into his office. I trekked down to corporate that day with little thought. *Perhaps a new opportunity coming my way? Maybe a new strategy to grow my region?*

I was directed to the conference room, where Bob met me. "Look, I am really sorry, but I am going to cut right to it. I have to let you go," Bob said.

"Ya, right. Quit messing with me, man. I have to get back to the office. I have a really busy day," I replied nonchalantly.

"No, I'm serious. I have to let you go." Bob didn't do well with confrontation and struggled to get those words out a second time. I could tell he wasn't messing around.

"OK," I said.

"OK? Is that all you have to say?" Bob asked.

"What do you want me to say? That I am your best sales guy? That I have consistently put up the best numbers in this place/ That you are crazy to let me go/ That cutting me loose will cost you? I could say all of those things, but it looks like your mind has already been made up."

"It is what it is," Bob finished.

Bob was a messenger. He honestly didn't have the backbone to argue corporate's request to lay me off. To corporate leadership, I was a number. But to Bob, and the regional office, I was an asset. Bob shouldn't have been in that leadership spot—I felt I should have. Leaders fight for their people and what's best for their team—they do not just take orders. But the company's top-tier executives had chosen Bob, and with that, I was gone.

As hard as it was to accept the fact that I had been laid off, Bob's words came with an overwhelming sense of peace. It didn't rock me at all. I grabbed my stuff and called Michelle. That was a hard conversation, but I conveyed the confidence that I felt: God was with us, and God would provide for and protect us. I was weak, helpless to control my situation. God was my strength, and that's all I needed.

Michelle believed that too, but the practical reality was still there. She cried, and why wouldn't she? We had a nine-year-old and two-year-old, a mortgage and other bills, and no additional sources of income. To make financial matters worse, we hadn't been smart about money. I made a very good income, but we were living far beyond our means and had little savings. We had made unnecessary upgrades to our house, went out to dinner too often, and drove cars that were nicer than we needed. Getting laid off meant we were going to quickly run out of money.

The money I made at ARC made it difficult to find comparable financial offers in the marketplace. More difficult was finding a company that did business in alignment with my personal values, which had been strengthened significantly in the five years since my faith conversion.

Within days of being laid off, a friend who'd left ARC two years prior called to let me know the company he now worked for—a competitor to ARC—was interested in bringing me on. They'd apparently been eyeing me for some time and knew the opportunity to recruit me was ripe. I'd never before considered working there, but I was open to the discussion because my friend worked there and he was happy.

I met with the owner, and after some negotiation, I took a sales position. The company was quite a bit behind in terms of technology and process, but the President and his leadership team were open to making changes to become more competitive. I was down for the challenge.

Unfortunately, after a few months, I realized they were not as open to change as they'd claimed—at least, not committed to doing it the right way. The company specifically targeted my former employer's clients, having encouraged other past employees to steal client lists. Also, choices were made to cut corners with some of the equipment used to produce jobs, leading to less than the best quality work. In addition, the owners were negotiating under-the-table deals with vendors and even employees. I wasn't down for that and left in November 2011.

I interviewed for various sales jobs, and though I was having good conversations, nothing felt right. After one specific interview, the vice president of sales of a large, well-known company offered me a position. I decided to call it quits—quits on interviewing, that is.

I told Michelle I'd been offered the job but that I didn't feel good about it. I was feeling led to start my own business. I didn't want to compromise my values or put clients in awkward positions—I wanted to sell the way I believed was right, and I wanted to better use my God-given gifts and talents. Michelle had every reason to say, "Heck, no! Get a real job!" She was a full-time stay-at-home mom, and we had five hundred dollars in our checking account with no savings.

We needed to fulfill our financial obligations—mortgage, utilities, car payments, insurance, and groceries. But Michelle never spoke a discouraging word. Instead, she said something that will forever be ingrained in me: "If you believe you can do it, I believe you can too, and I trust you."

Those words were all I needed to hear. She meant them, and I would do everything humanly possible to never let her down. Because my dad was an entrepreneur, and I'd heard from so many others of their entrepreneurial journeys, I knew I was in for a rough road. But I believed I had what it took in skill set and mindset. And I believed God would lead and guide me at every step, and provide for me and my family whether I could or not.

I anticipated the best I could, and yet, I wasn't ready for the journey I was about to embark on. Thankfully, God was!

ENTREPRENEURSHIP

Back when I worked for ARC, the company had a corporate sales trainer named Stan. Stan's amazing ability to teach us how to be better salespeople was eclipsed only by his respectable character as a man. I was captivated by what Stan did and how he did it. He was a master of his craft, always drawing us into his thinking, turning our focus on what was most important for success in our role, and helping us produce results from that learning.

Now that I was starting my business, I wanted to do what Stan did so well but for multiple companies. I planned to take all of my sales experience, coupled with what I'd learned from Stan—as well as from many of the nation's best sales trainers and sales programs—and create a business to help entrepreneurs, business owners, and salespeople achieve their sales goals. I would become a sales performance coach.

Starting a business can be pretty easy, but getting people to pay you money once you start that business is a whole different animal. I put my name out there in my business networks, spreading the word that I wanted to coach and train. I got some small bites but nothing big.

I had expected that, so I had an interim plan to generate income. Because I had spent so many years in the printing world with ARC, I called every business I had dealt with, offering to design and print their business cards, flyers, posters, stickers, T-shirts, and more. I then called a few vendors I knew and quickly established relationships in order to fulfill those orders. One early challenge was that profit margins in the print industry are not great. I was hustling, but I wasn't making a whole lot of money. Some jobs profited me three hundred dollars while others profited me as little as thirty bucks. I took anything I could get. My family needed a roof over their heads and food in their stomachs.

Being unable to provide for my family was emotionally tough and mentally frustrating. It brought back feelings of my upbringing and all the things we lacked. At times, it tempted me to doubt God's goodness. I wondered whether or not God had led me in the right direction.

All of this struggle soon took a hard toll on my self-image. Growing up, I was conditioned to be self-reliant. My mom, by way of my dad's departure, demonstrated every bit of what it meant to do all that was necessary to sustain herself and her family. Whenever my mom was sick or out of the house, I stepped into that role.

My dad was a go-getter and could figure out almost anything. He was very smart and super handy. Those parts of my dad rubbed off on me. The older I got, the more I believed I didn't need anyone to help me thrive.

That "I can do anything myself" belief came to a screeching halt midway through 2012. That year was the most financially difficult of my life. Some months, I made less than one thousand dollars. We cut back on every unnecessary expense, including dining out (unless we had a gift card) and vacations. I was working so hard to meet people, sell print work, and promote my sales coaching business, but I wasn't generating enough income. I prayed for God to bring me clients to serve so I wouldn't have to be so financially reliant on others. Michelle and I prayed together for the same, as did our friends in faith. All signs pointed to staying the course and not taking another job.

God was leading me down that path for a very specific reason. He needed to break me, to show me I couldn't do life on my own. He wanted me to see that relying on myself was another disaster waiting to happen. With self-reliance, I would work myself into the ground, resort to desperate, likely unethical, business practices to make money, and feel justified in spending less time with my family to put more into my business. That journey never ends well for me or anyone.

If all the thoughts, strategies, ideas, and even effort I put forth was coming up short in providing for my family and successfully building a business, what was I to do?

I needed to rely completely on God—that's what. As I did, God worked in ways I didn't expect and, frankly, didn't always like. A gift card for the local grocery store showed up on our front doorstep. An anonymous cashier's check to pay our tax bill found its way into our mailbox. In the beginning, I hated it. It felt so humiliating. But I had to accept help, and even ask for more at times. Otherwise, I would have to face the possibility of my family not having food or a home. Any pride I had left was broken. I felt inadequate, but I also rejoiced in my brokenness because it lifted more of the "I've got this" weight that had crushed me a few years prior.

Nevertheless, I couldn't wait for that season of life to be done. But that season forced me to run to God in ways I hadn't before. I spent all my free time reading God's word, praying, and surrounding myself with fellow Christians who could share His wisdom with me. In the Lord's Prayer, Jesus tells us to pray for "daily bread." I prayed, literally, for daily bread. I prayed God would bring a client—many clients, actually. I prayed that somehow God would allow my family to protect all we had gained up to that point.

TWO STEPS FORWARD, ONE STEP BACK

In March 2013, my prayers for professional fruit finally came to fruition. I landed some real coaching clients. During the first few months of the new year, I went from generating fifteen hundred to two thousand dollars per month in revenue to five thousand monthly. It was an amazing feeling. I was doing what I loved to do, and fully providing for my family through my business. I praised God every day. I praised Him not only for what He had done, but also for what He was doing moment by moment. I was regularly blown away by the opportunities He gave me and what I was able to do with them.

My business was consistently growing, and I was generating enough income to pay for our regular obligations. However, the financial hardships of the previous year had put me in a position in which I had gotten behind on a couple of credit card payments, and I could not always pay my mortgage or bills. A large majority of Americans were also struggling to pay their mortgages, so plenty of relief programs were available to homeowners like us to help during that time. Sometime in mid-2012, Michelle and I applied for a modification to our mortgage. It was a complex process that included interaction with three different lenders because that's how many times our mortgage was sold in a twelve-month period.

I cannot recount the number of phone calls, emails, and faxes I exchanged with the various lenders to provide the necessary information to show we could not afford our mortgage, but wanted to stay in our house. I provided documentation also to verify that for the previous eleven years I was never even one day late on a mortgage payment. But responses were mixed. Sometimes, a mortgage company representative assured me we could modify our loan. Other times, it seemed to be a complete impossibility. Someone on a Tuesday might tell me we were now making too much money to qualify for relief, and the following Thursday somebody else would say we didn't make enough money to qualify for the modified payment. *Talk about confusing!*

As I continued to battle with mortgage companies, we were also dealing with other hardships. Our air conditioning went out during the summer of 2013—one of the hottest summers on record in Southern California. Some nights it was ninety-five degrees inside our house, and our only reprieve was a portable air-conditioning unit in our primary bedroom. We made beds on the floor so the kids could sleep in the a/c as well.

Also, our pool was leaking water from a subsurface crack. We refilled it with water daily to keep the pool plaster from being exposed to direct sun. But after a few months, we couldn't keep up with it and had to let the pool drain. The crack was getting worse and we feared further subsurface damage. We didn't have the financial means to fix the crack, so we could no longer cool off in the pool.

Household issues, along with the outstanding financial obligations, continued to pour on. My sales coaching business was growing, but I still couldn't see a path out of the deep hole we were in. It was so stressful and deprived me of sleep at night. I strategized and planned, and I talked to anyone I could to find a way out. But, my fear of losing our home grew. I prayed, we prayed, day after day, begging God to allow us to stay in the house in which we were married and had raised our kids. I would have done anything to stay in that house. It was *our house*!

Eventually, we got the devastating news that the bank was foreclosing. Thankfully, I was doing some work for a real estate team that connected us with the right people who got our foreclosure changed to a short sale. The short sale would be kinder to our credit and also ease our transition from the home. That didn't change the fact that we were out of options and were losing the house we loved so much. I bawled my eyes out. We had to prepare to leave.

We had to figure out where to go and what we could afford. While I was earning a consistent income, we were still on a pretty tight budget. That made it hard to find a decent rental in our area. Trying to find another single-family house was completely out of the question. Instead, we looked for two-bedroom apartments we could squeeze into, trying to keep our kids in the school district. It was depressing, but Michelle and I pressed on, looking at every place we could to see what might work best for us.

Then, a miracle happened.

One Sunday afternoon in late September 2013, two months before we were set to move out of our house, we set up a bounce house for the kids and hosted a front yard barbecue for our church group and some neighbors. It was a way to stay connected to the community and, hopefully, share the gospel. But God was instead ready to share something with us.

Doug was a neighbor who lived across the street. We hadn't talked much over the years—typical SoCal suburban behavior—but our daughters were about the same age and played together from time to time. Doug and his wife had recently bought a new house elsewhere in the city. They had just moved out. Doug walked across the street during our barbecue to chitchat about our party, life, and what was going on. "So, have you guys thought about where you are going?" Doug asked.

"We aren't a hundred percent sure," I replied, "but we've been looking at two-bedroom apartments in the area."

"What's your budget?" he asked.

"Way less than you will get for your house—that's for sure," I said with a laugh.

"You never know," Doug said.

"Oh, I know. Don't worry about it, man."

Doug backed off of the house-related questions, and we enjoyed the barbecue a bit longer. As he was leaving, he said, "Hey, let's set up a time to grab lunch in the next couple of weeks."

"Uh, OK." I was surprised and curious, considering Doug and I had not ever spoken longer than fifteen minutes, never mind sharing a meal together. I didn't know what to expect when we met the following week.

We sat down and started with some small talk. "So, I know I asked before, but have you guys decided any further on what your plans will be for housing?" Doug asked. "What's your budget, exactly?"

"Between eighteen hundred and two thousand dollars a month," I said, knowing that was the budget for a stylish cardboard box but not a solid-structure dwelling.

"I can do that," Doug said without hesitation.

"You can do what?" I asked, puzzled.

"Eighteen hundred dollars."

"Eighteen hundred?" I exclaimed. "Are you nuts? That's crazy to even offer that, considering houses in our neighborhood are easily renting in the mid to high two-thousands."

"I understand," Doug said, "but I know your family, and we would much rather rent to a good family. Plus, I feel for your situation, and I want to make sure your kids can stay in their neighborhood and stay in the same schools."

My eyes welled up with tears. I couldn't believe this guy, whom I didn't know very well, was willing to do that. "Thank you," I said. "That is beyond kind and generous of you."

But it wasn't only Doug who made that offer. I am sure it was God. God knew we needed a place to stay, and maybe more important, God wanted us to have a soft landing from the brutal financial season we had been in. Many things were repossessed, credit cards were cut up, and we were on the verge of losing our house. But somehow, someway, God used this blessing to overshadow all of our hurt and struggle of the previous eighteen months.

I rushed home as fast as I could to tell Michelle the amazing news. We would only have to move across the street (and one house down). We could do it without financial strain. Michelle was in complete disbelief. That wasn't all—Doug offered to replace all the carpet in the house with whatever we chose, and he would do any small updates, including painting the inside how we wanted. Best of all, we could move in whenever we were ready and he treated our first month's rent as our security deposit so we didn't have to come up with any more out-of-pocket money.

We moved in November 2013. It was difficult to leave the home we'd bought together and raised our kids in. To walk away from the abundance of blood, sweat, and tears we had put into making that house our home. But the move was also joy-filled. We gained new floors, new paint, a perfectly working central a/c unit, and a new season of life.

APPLYING THE WOUND-ANALYSIS FRAMEWORK

This season of trials and tribulations beat me up and brought me to some of my weakest moments, causing me to doubt myself immensely. I didn't like the struggles. Who does? But I came to understand God was showing me that apart from Him I am powerless. Though I had been battered, I needed those times to see just how important it is to rely on God for everything. God knew all along the wounds, like all those before, would be used for my good.

Acknowledge the hurt.

This wound of failure was the result of getting laid off from my high-paying job, struggling to get my business off the ground, and short-selling our house.

Realize the effect.

The wound of failure hurt me in two major ways:

1. Getting laid off, struggling with my business, and short-selling our house came with shame and embarrassment. It was hard to tell those stories because I felt they made me look bad. I hated that.

2. Each struggle cast doubt over my potential to be a future success. I wasn't sure if I would ever be successful again, and honestly, I thought maybe my financial struggle was a punishment from God for the bad I had done earlier in my life.

Unlock the greatness.

These dark days were hard, but God used the wound of failure to strengthen me in three major ways:

1. God showed me what matters most. Driving nice cars, wearing expensive watches, and owning a house in a high-dollar zip code used to mean a lot to me. I still think that stuff is great, but it's not everything. When we lost all that, my wife and I committed to each other that regardless of what we had or where we lived, being together was all that mattered.

2. Later in my faith journey, I understood that God doesn't hold against us our sins of the past. I focused too much on money, spent money irresponsibly, and let money drive a wedge into my marriage. When Jesus said on the cross, "It is finished," he meant it. He meant that the penalty for every sin His people, such as me, ever committed or will ever commit, has been paid for *in full*. Yes, we will still face consequences for our actions in this world. But He will not hold those against us. For me, that meant I might experience wealth again without fear that God would hold it back.

3. God taught me to rely on others—a 180-degree shift from my days of complete self-reliance. When we were struggling financially, our closest family and friends stepped in to help with whatever we needed. The obvious benefit may be that I opened up to practical help in times of need. Beyond that, and more important, I saw the blessing of having people who care about me—not about my house or my car or my money, but me. I finally felt fully accepted for who I was. This continues to be a huge blessing.

All in all, the wound of failure enabled me to see that, whether I'm acting as a husband, father, friend, or business owner, valuing people is the key to greatness. When we lost our home, we were blessed with a wonderful place to live by a generous family. After being laid off from my job and struggling to get my business off the ground, I eventually succeeded. I recently celebrated eleven years of consulting for dozens of businesses, coaching hundreds of individuals, and speaking to thousands of people. Through the wound of failure, I've helped all those individuals make more money, live more fulfilling lives, and impact the world in ways they have been called to.

Healing the wound of failure and recognizing the value of relationships led me to repair my most broken relationship of all—the one with my dad.

7

WOUNDED BY UNFORGIVENESS

MARCH 18, 2001, THE DAY MICHELLE AND I GOT MARRIED, WAS THE last time I would speak to my father for nearly ten years.

A few months prior, we had two pretty big disagreements. One was related to business I did with a friend of his when the deal went sideways over unrealistic expectations on the friend's part. The other disagreement had to do with an insurance company that took my money but claimed I never paid them—my policy was canceled, negatively affecting the car loan my dad cosigned for me. Instead of hearing me out, my dad took the other people's sides in both cases. I am not saying I was blameless, but past feelings of anger and hurt boiled back up and once again affected my relationship with my dad.

By the time Michelle and I were wedding planning, I didn't want to invite my dad. I was deeply hurt and didn't know how else to deal with it. Michelle was adamant about inviting my dad to our wedding, but she also wanted to be supportive of me because she knew how hurt I was. We talked often about the effects of my dad leaving when I was young, about me having to run away from his home at one point, and even about the recent issues.

My mom, meantime, wouldn't accept not having my dad at my wedding. She shared with me multiple times the importance of including my dad. The irony of my mom pressing to invite my dad was that she had every reason to want him excluded. Though they had been divorced for fifteen years, I am sure some hurt was still there. On top of that, my dad wasn't always the kindest to my mom. My mom was no peach either, but that wasn't an excuse for my dad to make my mom's life hard. With all that in mind, she was willing to look past that to ensure he was a part of my special day.

With the heavy influence from my soon-to-be wife and my mom, I agreed to invite my dad to the wedding. But as I revisited my parent's divorce, and how it affected me and my little brother growing up, I grew very angry. I was angry that when my dad left, we no longer had a man in our house. I tried to be that man, but dammit, I was six years old. I was angry that when my dad left, we had a roof over our heads but a lot of debt. My mom could work only so many jobs to provide for us.

Then something deeper and darker than the anger from his absence surfaced. I was angry at the fact that I'd spent seventeen years trying to prove to everyone that I was good enough. As a result, I made stupid decisions to fit in with the in-crowd, attempted to prove myself by fighting alongside my friends (which I wasn't very good at), and had a damaging hookup rampage from ages nineteen to twenty-two. Look, I take responsibility for all of my choices. But the open wound of being abandoned at six years old had festered into a series of bad decisions. That pissed me off.

I didn't know how to address my anger with my dad. He was intimidating, a strong guy with strict discipline and a heavy hand. So, I just cut him off. I waited until after the wedding because that was Michelle's and my night, so I wasn't going to take the attention away from our celebration. Throughout the wedding and reception,

I was around my dad and acknowledged him. I even hugged him goodbye at the end of the night. But that was the last time I hugged my dad for quite some time.

PARTIAL FORGIVENESS

As days, weeks, months, and years passed, a callus formed on my heart, leading me to care less and less about being separated from my dad. He was out of sight and out of mind. And his absence from my present life magnified his absence from my past. In large part, my decision to distance myself from him had made me angrier and more calloused. It became a vicious cycle.

By 2007, approximately six years into our separation, my dad was leaving messages on our home answering machine, asking me to pick up the phone to talk to him. That went on for years. Though he wept, I disregarded his cries for reconnection. I felt I was justified. He had hurt me so badly, so many times. I felt I didn't owe him anything. I believed he no longer had the right to be in my life.

But, as with everything else, God had a better plan. In October 2008, seven years since I'd last spoken to my father, I was up in Lake Arrowhead, California, at a Christian men's retreat. All sessions were held in a small performance hall, which was decorated like a mountain cabin. The atmosphere was electric as more than 150 men gathered to grow in faith, grow as men, grow as husbands and fathers, and outwardly worship God all weekend. I had never experienced anything like it, and to say I was overwhelmed would be an understatement. But that was the perfect setting for God to work. I was in God's creation, surrounded by brothers in the Lord.

I was two years into my faith and still learning a lot about God and myself—and how God related to me. Part of my expectation for that weekend was the hope that I would learn to be a better man alongside a lot of amazing men.

The most unexpected, yet powerful, moment came during the Saturday evening session. The guest speaker preached from the Bible, tying it all back to the idea that unforgiveness is often at the heart of harbored hurt, anger, and even sin in our lives. As he closed his message, he asked all of the men in the room to yell out something that resonated from his message—anything we needed God to help us heal from.

It hit me at once like a ton of bricks. I yelled out, "Unforgiveness!"

I had spent the past two years finding a new level of joy as the result of coming to understand that Jesus Christ died to forgive me of my sins. And yet, I held an enormous sense of unforgiveness toward my dad. Unforgiveness spreads like a terrible weed. Unforgiveness toward my dad made it easier for me to justify not forgiving others I felt had hurt me. Even worse was how it spread to sinful actions. Closing myself off meant I didn't have a good grasp of the meaning of forgiveness. When I lost my temper with my wife or punished my kids in excess of what they needed, I was realizing sin and its way of mirroring my dad's behaviors from my childhood. Instead of owning my actions and asking for forgiveness, I brushed them off or deflected them.

Then a thought became so clear it felt palpable: *How dare I accept the forgiveness Christ offered me—or ask for more of it—without extending it to others, especially someone as close as my dad?*

I broke. I fell to my knees and wept. A few guys came around me, concerned. They wanted to know what was going on, and I shared with them what I was feeling. They invited me to step outside and go deeper. We went back to one of the rooms to pray.

I asked God to show me what forgiveness would look like. I wanted to know how I could forgive someone who had hurt me so badly—someone I had pushed so far away that I had all but forgotten him. With the guys surrounding me, I said out loud, "Dad, I forgive you for everything you did and everything that happened between us from the time I was six years old to the present day." It felt so freeing to say that. As I said it, my buddies grabbed hold of me and hugged me, comforting me in my vulnerability.

I didn't know exactly what that type of forgiveness—the kind that truly wipes always the deepest of hurt—was to look like in a practical sense, but deep inside my heart, I believed I had taken the action I needed. I left the mountain, thinking I had done everything necessary, without any regard for actually contacting my dad. *Forgiveness in my heart is enough*, I thought.

For the next few months, I believed I could finally put it all past me. I was sorely mistaken. Older and wiser men in my weekly Bible study, those in our group of young married couples, and even the pastors I had befriended were sharing with me that forgiveness involves more than saying it to myself or even to God. I'd rejoiced with them all about my mountaintop experience, and while they were happy for me, they also encouraged me to take some sort of action toward forgiving my dad. I heard over and over again that I had to extend that forgiveness to my dad. I couldn't just keep it inside my heart. I decided to write him a letter in early 2009.

At first, I didn't know what to say or how to say it. I needed him to understand my pain from all the ways he had hurt me. I didn't want it to be full of anger and rage. God had healed me of that. I was scared and nervous to send the letter. Part of those feelings were the result of residual fear of my dad and the possibility of a negative reaction. But if I am honest, I was even more afraid of what would happen if he responded positively. I definitely wasn't ready for that.

I put pen to paper and began to write. My feelings surfaced and poured out onto that paper. I wanted to share all of this with my dad so he knew that, before I could forgive him, I needed to be forgiven by God and learn what God's forgiveness means.

Dad,

Up until seven months ago, I really had no desire to write this letter or even communicate with you.

Then in October of last year I was at a weekend men's retreat with a group of about 150 guys from our church. During one of our sessions, we were asked to close our eyes and, when we felt the urge, yell out something we needed God's help with. It began, and every problem someone could have was yelled out: greed, lust, better father, better husband, honesty.

When that urge finally hit me, I could have claimed any one of those things along with many others, but God pushed the word "unforgiveness" out of me.

At first, I didn't quite get it. But as that day and weekend wore on, I began to realize that here I was, living a whole new life with God. I had given my life to Him a few years prior, and while I had worked so hard to become a better father, a better husband, and a better person, I still wasn't working on all of it.

It has taken me from October until now to really put these thoughts together. I have really struggled, because I thought my forgiveness would have been hollow. I could say the words but not completely mean it. I have talked with a few different people, and with their advice and God's guidance, I realized that for me to begin my walk with the Lord, I had to ask for forgiveness for so much. I had to open myself up to anything and everything I did and shouldn't have done.

So here goes....

- *I forgive you for leaving us kids at such a young age for very selfish reasons. Looking back, I honestly believe it was the very best thing that could have happened to mom, Cory, and me, but boy was it tough.*

- *I forgive you for putting us in bad spots time and time again when we were young. To spite mom, you made sure we had just about everything we wanted when we were with you, only to suffer daily at home as mom struggled to juggle multiple jobs to provide food and a house for us to grow up in.*

- *I forgive you for all the bad things you said about our mom. The name-calling and bad-mouthing made me lose a lot of respect for you. Just because you guys could not work out your differences as a married couple didn't mean you had to disrespect a woman who worked so hard to raise your kids the best way she could.*

- *I forgive you for making Cory an outcast. Some extremely tough events happened throughout his childhood, and some seemed too hard to accept, but he is still your child. To this day, he struggles with some of the ill-hearted comments and negativity directed at him, and nobody deserves that.*

- *I forgive you for making me sneak away early one morning because the life I was living just wasn't the way I wanted to finish high school. I tried so hard to approach you in a responsible way and you shut me out. I wasn't running from anything, just trying to be a kid.*

I hope you understand that in no way did I write this letter to judge, convict, or hurt you. I want to be able to look at myself and know I did for others what I constantly ask God to do for me.

I am not exactly sure what happens from here. So much time has passed and so many things have changed in my life that I have no idea what the future holds. If there is to be any communication past this, I think a letter or email is best for me right now. There may be a day when that changes, but it will take some time.

I hope all is well with you, Madeline, and the rest of the family out there.

Ryan

I would be lying if I were to say writing that letter was all about forgiveness. I was never able to share my feelings with him before and felt this was as good a time as any. He fulfilled my request, never attempting to reply or reach back out. Much later, I understood how kind it was of him to give me the space even though he so deeply wanted to reconnect. While I have no regrets about sending that letter to my dad, or saying the things I said, it definitely hurts now to read it because I am certain it hurt my dad. By God's grace, my dad and I eventually would take every step necessary to be closer than we ever had.

RECONCILIATION

In October 2009, I ended up back at that same men's retreat in Lake Arrowhead—another awesome weekend to connect with more men in the church. After the previous year's retreat, I was expecting God to once again move in a profound and transformational way. But what that was, I wasn't completely sure.

During prayer time after a speaker session, something happened. There were no prompts to proclaim harbored anger or hurt. Nobody told me it was time to go deeper into exploring what God wanted me to do. Still, I felt something. Something was off—it wasn't right. As I prayed, something inside of me "told me" the forgiveness I had extended to my dad a year prior—by writing a letter that denied his ability to respond—wasn't complete. Such a letter needed to be more meaningful and even practical.

I recalled these words of the Apostle Paul: "Be kind to one another, tenderhearted, forgiving one another, as God in Christ forgave you." Forgiving others, "as Christ forgave you," is quite a task.

When Jesus says, "You are forgiven, He definitely wipes the slate clean, but he also goes far beyond that. He enters right back into a relationship with you, as if nothing had ever happened in the first place. While I would never claim to be as perfect as God, I strive to replicate as closely as possible the forgiveness He extends to me. I prayed, and I sought biblical counsel to figure out how to truly forgive my dad in the way God was surely asking me to.

After months of thought, prayer, and discussion with others, I sent my dad another email, this time inviting him to get together. I was nervous and anxious, but also excited about the possibilities God had in store. I shared with my dad in that email that, for the time being, I wanted to meet only with him—no other family members involved. I also shared with him that I was hopeful we could go into that meeting with a relatively clean slate. It wasn't as if we could ignore this huge gap in our lives or past hurts, but if we had any chance of a renewed relationship, we couldn't let those issues hang over our heads.

My dad and stepmom by now were living in Arizona, so we coordinated a meetup at BJ's Restaurant and Brewhouse in Menifee, California. Few moments from my past are as clear as that one. Driving there, I was nervous and scared. I had so many questions running through my mind: *What is going to happen? What are we actually going to say? Will he be mad at me? How awkward is this going to be?* I blared worship music in my car, hoping God would bring me some peace and give us both the words to best enter back into a relationship.

Shaking, I walked into the restaurant. It was filled with the voices and laughter of a busy lunch crowd. Through the crowd, I saw my dad sitting at a table in the bar area. He was as recognizable as always, but I also saw nervousness on his face. I felt more at peace to know we were both in a similar state of mind. We made eye contact, and he got up from the table. A huge smile on his face and tears in his eyes, he walked toward me. We embraced in what was the best hug we'd ever shared—perfectly welcoming, warm, and safe. All of my nervousness and fears faded away. I was exactly where my heart needed to be.

We sat down and just talked. While it was impossible to totally dismiss the decade-long gap, we connected on some level as if we had never missed a moment. He asked about Michelle, the kids, my job, and what I had been up to. I asked about my stepmom, my brothers and their families, and what he did for fun. I shared with him how God had moved in my life and how so much of what God did in my heart led me to open my heart to my dad. What never got brought up was the past hurt. It was obviously there, but I knew that I didn't need to bring any of that into this new season of life with my dad. It was unnecessary for our future. And from the way that my dad talked to and treated me, I was sure that he didn't want to engage in any of that past hurt either. It was amazing! And I know that it was all the work of God.

Before we left, we discussed getting together again. My dad and stepmom would be at my aunt and uncle's house in Menifee in a few weeks. That's where we would all meet—my dad and stepmom, Michelle and the girls, and my aunt and uncle. I'd missed my stepmom, aunt, and uncle so much over the years, so I was excited.

The nervous excitement kicked in as we pulled up to my aunt and uncle's house. I was excited to see everyone but nervous because I wasn't sure if any animosity or awkward feelings from all the time apart might cast a shadow on the reunion. We let Chloe knock on the door—two-year-old kids are great icebreakers in the face of uncertain encounters. My aunt opened the door, and the tears flowed immediately. I hugged her, and then tightly hugged my stepmom. I'd missed her immensely and was so happy to see her. This was also the first time for my parents, aunt, and uncle to meet the kids. The joy and love overwhelmed in the best of ways. We caught up, told stories, and laughed, just like old times.

While Michelle and I talked about our journey to faith and all the work God was doing in our lives, my stepmom got up from the couch to come over and embrace me. "I have been praying for this every single day," she said through tears. "God answered my prayers." I felt that not only had forgiveness come to full fruition, but also that God was at work in mighty ways and was showing himself to be *so* good to me and all of my family.

From that day, we connected more deeply with my dad, my stepmom, and my stepbrothers and their families. We took trips to Arizona, where they all lived, and they made trips to California to spend time with us. My dad and I talked on the phone pretty regularly, which was so cool for me. Because it had been ten years since we'd had any relationship, this was the first time that, as a mature man, I had my dad in my life for advice and guidance—whether to figure out how to wire something in the house or decide on a new business opportunity. I had missed out for so long and was trying to make up for the lost time.

Today, I consider my dad to be a best friend. I love him so much, and I see him as often as I can. Even as I write this chapter, I am on a plane to Arizona to spend two days with my dad, stepmom, and one of my stepbrothers. I can't wait to get there, hug them, and see what God has planned for us for the next couple of days.

APPLYING THE WOUND-ANALYSIS FRAMEWORK

I had thought my wedding would be the last time I would ever see my dad. I was so hurt and angry that it didn't seem possible for us to reconcile. But in God's kindness, through His work in my life, He made a way for something even better than reconciliation. God gave me and my dad the incredible relationship we never had but always needed. Further, the Wound Analysis Framework helped me more clearly understand all that happened between my dad and me—from the time of my parents' divorce in 1984 to our 2011 reconciliation—and how to become a better man myself because of it all.

Acknowledge the hurt.

The wound of unforgiveness was the result of decades of hurt from my relationship with my dad. While that wound started with my parents' divorce in 1984, I still believe he could have worked to repent and restore what was broken. It felt like he instead made it deliberately worse until I couldn't take any more and had to completely cut off our relationship in 2001.

Realize the effect.

The wound of unforgiveness affected me in two major ways:

1. Unforgiveness caused me to be angry, resentful, and bitter toward my dad. As a result, I risked the possibility of never again having a relationship with him. If he had unexpectedly passed away, I would not have been able to say "I am sorry," "I forgive you," or "I love you." I would not have been able to hug him, learn from him, or hang out with him again.

2. Unforgiveness also caused me to be angry, resentful, and bitter toward other people and in other relationships in my

life. Unforgiveness doesn't affect only the one I haven't forgiven. It tends to affect everyone and everything else around me like a toxic poison.

Unlock the greatness.

God used the wound of unforgiveness to strengthen me in two major ways:

1. God helped bring my dad and me back together for an even better relationship. Reconnecting with my dad made me a better man. He's shared so much wisdom with me and taught me so many practical things. He is always there to offer his advice without judgment, though he is clear that he expects the best from me because he wants the best for me. I love my dad, and I try to talk to and spend as much time with him as I can.

2. Through the process of forgiveness, I learned that while I can disagree all day long with what my dad did or how he did it, I should never expect him to be perfect. It wouldn't be fair. God is the only perfect Father. When the time came for me to be a father, in trying to do my best every day, I never projected perfection but instead pointed my kids to the One who is.

Restoring my relationship with my dad was one of God's greatest gifts God to me. Beyond the obvious—having him in my life and my family's life, turning to him for advice, and feeling a deep love from him and toward him—healing that wound also helped me endure new professional wounds that were coming.

8

WOUNDED BY UNFAIR ACCUSATIONS

THE YEAR 2014 BEGAN IN A WAY I HADN'T EXPERIENCED IN A WHILE— everything in my life was good. Michelle and I were doing fantastic, my relationship with my dad was amazing, I was pastoring a church that was slowly growing, and my three-year-*young* coaching business was strong. I was working exclusively with business owners, entrepreneurs, and sales pros, helping them optimize growth and potential through business strategy, mindset, and human behavior. Most of my coaching was in-person, one-to-one with the individual, though I was also asked to lead corporate workshops and group trainings. The best part was that my work produced significant financial results for my clients, in turn enabling me to consistently earn more than ten thousand dollars each month.

Earning that amount of money ensured that I stay in front of all of our bills, out of all debt, and in a place that allowed my family to enjoy more frequent nights out and even some small vacations. It was a big step for us after so much struggle, offering a sense of relief and comfort I had not felt in six years.

But what I didn't plan for as I achieved success was the challenge in producing more of it. Being busy with clients was awesome, but that also meant I wasn't doing enough prospecting to fill my pipeline. That was definitely a cobbler-without-shoes error that caught up to me. Midway through the year, situations with two major clients left a huge gap in my revenue. I was scared that our family could quickly fall back into the state we were in during 2012, without enough money to even pay our bills.

I was blessed to have a great friend who referred two new clients my way. One in particular, The Centennial Group, a health insurance brokerage in Orange County, was about to make a very unexpected proposition. In April 2015, I received a call from the COO while she was traveling for a conference. "Hey, Ryan, it's Vickie. How are you?"

"Hey, Vickie! I'm great. How's the conference going?"

"Really good, actually, which is why I want to talk to you. Matt [Centennial's CEO] and I were talking, and we've decided that we need to hire a full-time sales leader to manage the sales department. As you know, I have been doing that myself, but with the growth we are expecting, I need to be more focused on my role, and we need someone to focus more on the sales leadership role. After talking with Matt, we feel like you are the best person fit for that role. What do you think?"

"Wow, Vickie. I am really honored you would consider me. As you can tell, I am quite surprised and will definitely need to think about it."

"No problem," she said. "I just wanted to let you know where we are with this. We can talk more when you're on-site next week."

While I was grateful, I wasn't at all prepared to consider such an offer. I was happily running my business, and on top of that, I was pastoring the church and committed to spending a few days a week on that outside of Sunday mornings. Vickie and Matt told me to take some time to think about it and to get back to them. Then, a few weeks later, they gave me an ultimatum. The COO was ready to pull the trigger and needed to know if I was accepting the role or if they needed to recruit elsewhere.

I needed to take the offer a little bit more seriously and bring it to my wife. My wife was always 100-percent behind me in every decision I made, especially when it came to the business. She trusted I would do what was right to best provide for our family, and this was no exception. My wife and I discussed what it would mean to have the stability of working for a solid organization with good values and a lot of future potential.

The process of considering Centennial's offer was quite challenging. I was confident God had called me to start my coaching business back in 2011, and I didn't feel Him calling me to stop coaching. At the same time, I believed God would honor a decision to steadily provide for my family. I was grateful that options were being presented, but I was definitely in a tough spot.

In May 2015, I officially accepted the role as director of sales and marketing for The Centennial Group. In the back of my mind, I was figuring I would spend the next seven to ten years there, supporting them in achieving some amazing goals, and then go back into business as a coach and consultant. But like every other plan we make for ourselves, God ultimately decides what happens and when.

The next two years proved I was indeed called by God to take the job at Centennial. But it also proved that job to be a temporary position.

A CHALLENGING SEASON

My first year working for The Centennial Group was amazing. It had its fair share of challenges, but all in all, it felt great to be part of a team on a mission to do good and achieve success in the process.

I got along well with Matt, CEO, and Vickie, COO. I was building rapport with the existing sales team, while hiring new people to build onto that team.

Unfortunately, the good days at this company didn't last long. October 2016 included two major events that rattled our organization.

The first was the resignation of our top salesperson. Our team was built around him, and he truly was one of a kind. He had his rough edges, but what he had already produced in his career coupled with his future potential made him somebody any organization could ride off into the sunset with. When he left, not only did a large amount of revenue go along with him, but his departure also cracked the trust we had on our leadership team, and the culture of the company was changed forever.

The second event was far more heartbreaking. My direct counterpart, who led our client service team, was a thirty-year-old superstar with a world of opportunity in front of her. Unfortunately, a lifetime of achievement and high expectations all but set her up for failure. Nobody set the bar higher than she did herself, and when she couldn't meet the challenges, nobody was harder on her than she was. Over a period of about six months, we watched her slowly deteriorate through a brutal mental health battle. As much as we loved and supported her, it wasn't enough to get her out of her own head. She was seeing various medical professionals who were more interested in prescribing medication than in healing her mind. In mid-October, she made the decision to end her life.

Both of those events rattled our organization to its core. As a business, we were dealing with the loss of significant amounts of revenue, and as people, we were experiencing the heartbreak of losing somebody we cared so much about. Our goal as a leadership team was to do everything to support all of our employees who were affected and try to help them move forward. It wasn't easy, and the company culture never was quite the same.

Turning the corner from 2016 to 2017 should have presented an opportunity for a breath of fresh air for us all, and in some ways it did. Our CEO decided to join other like-minded CEOs across the country in forming a national organization. It would create a lot of wonderful growth opportunities and possibilities for the company as a whole, while also having the potential to positively impact all of the employees.

But as I had seen ten years prior when working for a large public corporation, such a decision usually includes its fair share of battles. The more we wore into 2017, the more unsettled I felt in my role. Our sales team was not doing great. Some aspects of that were the team's fault, such as lazy efforts toward new business development. Other aspects were my responsibility as their leader, such as failing to hold them more accountable to the metrics they needed to hit. And yet other aspects were the negative effects of decisions made from farther up the food chain, mostly related to corporate bureaucracy.

The corporate challenges affected our ability to act autonomously and negatively impacted forward momentum. Tension increased among our leadership team, and it just wasn't much fun anymore. I engaged in heated discussions with my bosses, very uncharacteristic of what our relationship was in the past. One such discussion got particularly heated with my boss, Vickie. While I do not recall the specific issue, I clearly remember it was the first time in the two years I worked there that she and I had ever raised our voices at each other. Business isn't always rainbows and unicorns, and there will be challenging seasons, but something was particularly off and I struggled more and more to keep my footing.

I had discussions with a few friends and other people close to me about whether or not I should continue in that role. I prayed, but I wasn't hearing anything specific from God on what to do. With no clear sign, I chose to forge on and avoid immediate changes. Little did I know that the sign I was about to receive would be extreme: the mass shooting in Las Vegas.

A CALL TO RETURN

On October 1, 2017, the mass shooting at the Route 91 Harvest music festival sent shockwaves through every facet of my life. I lost a close friend, nearly lost my wife, and had the sights and sounds of a war zone baked into my mind forever. I lost sleep, battled anxiety, and called into question everything I was doing in my life.

All of this brings us back to that moment in the first chapter of this book: me, alone in my office at Centennial, a few weeks after the shooting. I turned to stare out the floor-to-ceiling window that faced the coast of Newport Beach. An overwhelming feeling came over me and, with it, this question: *What in the hell am I doing with my life?*

The more I pondered that and prayed over it, the greater my realization that God was leading me to reevaluate who I was and what I was doing in every area of my life. Yes, I was happy, healthy, and successful, but what matters most to God is that I live my life to His glory. I believed part of that required me to live as the person, and in the roles, He specifically called me to.

I set off on a journey with my executive coach (someone who works with individuals in leadership roles within organizations to help them improve their skills, performance, and overall effectiveness), my wife, the other two pastors of our church, and a few close friends to answer for myself the following questions of utmost importance:

1. *Who am I?*

2. *Why am I here on this earth?*

3. *How does what happened to me help me become the greatest I possibly can be?*

For the next seven months I met with friends, family members, pastors, and anyone else close to me for advice. I prayed with them, and I repeatedly asked God what I was supposed to be doing. Some days, it seemed very clear, but others, so cloudy. At times, I felt ready to resign from my position and start coaching, while other days that felt hasty and irresponsible. I battled through thoughts that the Route 91 tragedy clouded some sense of myself, and I didn't want to overreact because of it. I struggled with the tension of choosing between the contentment and complacency of staying at Centennial versus the fear of stepping back into my coaching business and, in some sense, starting over.

I journaled quite extensively during that time. Here, I share some of those entries to demonstrate how desperate I was to answer the questions I was wrestling with. These are a few of those excerpts:

10/23/17 I don't want to waste my life pursuing good. I want to be great, or excellent.

10/31/17 I can't control most of the stress I receive, but what I can control I must focus on.

11/03/17 I can be better at everything I do, and better than most people by working harder and not allowing negativity to sink in.

12/12/17 I don't want to wake up one day and realize I've wasted my life being comfortable and predictable. I want to get after it. I want to take risks.

12/18/17 Life is hard. Even when the trials subside, the busyness and frustration make some days difficult to get through. I need to get back to being really clear about what I'm pursuing and what is standing in my way.

02/20/18 There are so many good things happening, but they seem to be covered by a dark cloud. I don't want to live life this way. I am scared. What now? I give 100 percent. What's next? I just don't know.

Every time I had a discussion about this crossroads in my life, I was completely transparent in sharing my thoughts with friends or family members. I wanted those closest to me to challenge everything I was thinking, because to best answer my deeply troubling question, "what the hell am I doing with my life?", I needed objective clarity and godly wisdom.

Even with my inner tug-of-war, I was intent on continuing to be a positive contribution to the organization I worked for. To start 2018, I conducted our most productive goal-planning meeting and sales kickoff ever. Gaining the buy-in of every sales rep, I had them more excited to chase their goals than I'd seen since leading the team.

I built some new sales processes to help the team set more appointments, as well as a new recruiting, hiring, and onboarding process that brought in a few young, promising business development reps. I believed these new processes would be very helpful in reaching our goals. While the struggles we experienced as a sales team before October 2017 still existed, I was committed to overcoming them. With all my heart, I wanted my team—and the organization—to be successful.

At times, though, it seemed as though Satan himself were piling on the attacks in hopes I would completely lose my mind.

UNFAIR ACCUSATIONS

One of those attacks came by way of fractured relationships with my bosses. We communicated respectfully and did not display anger to one another, but I was being treated differently and it really sucked. One specific instance absolutely broke my heart.

Matt and Vickie had invited me out to lunch, and I definitely expected a hard discussion—about my team's numbers and pinpointing why they came up short of their 2017 goal, as well as why salespeople still struggled through the beginning of 2018. Instead, the discussion quickly turned into an awkward blame game.

"Vickie and I feel like you are checked out," Matt said.

I was taken aback and frustrated by his comment, but I didn't want to project anger. I quickly collected myself. "Checked out? I have been working so hard to get the team back on track."

"We don't see it that way," Matt said. "While we obviously understand, we feel like you changed after Route 91."

Changed—are you fucking kidding me? I had been through hell, my friend was killed, and my life was torn to pieces in a flash of rapid gunfire. Of course, I had changed. Every morning was a fight to get up and give it my all. I had to intentionally put aside my grief and focus on being present for others. But I hadn't changed in the way Matt was implying. I was so pissed that I had a hard time saying anything. I asked, "Changed how?"

"You just seem like you are not as invested into us anymore, and you aren't getting the best results," Matt said.

No shit, I thought. We'd lost our best sales guy in late 2016 and never recovered, and we were struggling to hire quality talent because our compensation model was not comparable to our competitors.

"Matt, of course that was hard for me, but I have shown up every single day and given this company my all. I've worked as hard as possible to achieve success. If that's not good enough, then I don't know what else to say to you guys," I said.

Nothing was resolved at lunch, and we headed back to the office. That accusation hurt. I agree that our sales numbers were off, and I even agree that I could always do better (can't we all?). But they were so far off to characterize our lack of sales as a result of my being "checked out." As God is my witness, I was doing everything I could to steer that sales ship in the right direction. But Matt and Vickie didn't "see it that way."

That discussion—really, that specific statement—with all of my prayer time and conversations with friends and family over the previous months, brought me to the conclusion that I was no longer where I was supposed to be. As soon as that clicked in my mind, it became clear that my call was to coach again.

I don't regret taking the job at Centennial. I loved the good times with Matt, Vickie, and the rest of the team, and learned a lot from them. I was grateful for the income and what it provided for my family. And through specific moments, like the aftermath of the death of my coworker, I could see that God had me there to pray for and encourage others.

The decision to resign came with its fair share of challenges. I had to face my boss, Vickie, and break the news, which wouldn't be easy. While there was some tension between us, together we had fought battles, endured challenges, and rejoiced in wins. I also had to figure out how I would provide for my family.

The resignation conversation took place in May 2018. I was surprised at how well it went with Vickie, though we both shed some tears. I offered to give some time for the company to plan for my departure, so we agreed on a date nearly a month out. Most of that prep happened behind the scenes and without the knowledge of my sales team, or anyone else in the company, as Matt and Vickie were very concerned about the optics of my leaving.

They were so concerned with how it might look that I didn't get a send-off. On my last day, I packed my personal belongings, said a few goodbyes, and walked out that door for the last time. "I caught wind of some untrue rumors about my resignation, but I've left that drama behind me and choose not to rehash it."

As that drama was put behind me, God continued to affirm my decision to go forward. Two days after I resigned, I received a call from a prominent figure in the insurance business. The call ended with an agreement to immediately begin consulting and coaching for his organization. I received another call from an old friend who opened up a door to begin in-person consulting and coaching for a local firm that manufactured and distributed medical products. Between those two calls, I had exceeded my monthly income from my former job not two weeks after resigning. Throughout the remainder of 2018, I would eclipse that, making the most money I had ever made in a year.

Money is far from being the most important factor, and money had nothing to do with why I resumed coaching. But the financial success further solidified my decision. Beyond financial success, I was happier and more fulfilled. I loved the people I was working with and the work I was doing with them.

APPLYING THE WOUND-ANALYSIS FRAMEWORK

Though my professional life had been quite the roller-coaster ride from 2011 to 2014, I never expected some of the most emotionally stomach-churning drops to come later in my career, especially since I was working at a steady, successful company. With God's help, I used those challenges to become stronger professionally, personally, and spiritually.

Acknowledge the hurt.

The wound of unfair accusations came from my time at Centennial, as I didn't deserve to be held solely accountable for the company's lack of sales performance. It was never the result of my being "checked out," but that accusation hurt me, as did some of the treatment I received during a time when I was invested in and positively contributing to the organization.

Realize the effect.

Being falsely accused hurt me, not only because the claims weren't true but also because the accusations came from people I cared about and trusted. I take responsibility for my mistakes and missteps, but piling all the blame on me was misdirected and only further hindered company goals.

Unlock the greatness.

While the stretch of time from October 2016 to May 2018 was extremely difficult, it helped push me back toward God's higher calling in my life.

Professionally, my higher calling was to coach organizations and individuals to achieve the success they desired. Personally, my higher calling was to help people unlock their greatness and utilize that to be the best version of who God created them to be. Both of these callings became clear through that season, but they were honed and strengthened as I went through my process of development. One of the most powerful dynamics I've discovered on my journey is that when people are at their best, not only are their lives emotionally, relationally, spiritually, and even financially better, but they also perform better in their professional roles for the organizations they serve. While the best systems and processes in the world cannot make up for broken people in professional roles, the best people can make up for broken systems and processes. Better yet is when I get to develop both!

I've been gifted with the opportunity to pour myself out into every person God brings to me, and I am grateful that the wound of unfair accusations paved the way for me to see that. As important as it was for me to find more fulfillment in my professional life, church life was an even higher priority. Like most roles in life, that of a pastor can bring great joy and even greater pain.

9

WOUNDED BY CHURCH

WHEN I BECAME A CHRISTIAN IN 2006, I DID NOT IMAGINE I WOULD end up on a mission trip in a third-world country. But God was preparing my heart, because just more than four years later, one of our pastors announced a mission trip to Haiti, and I almost immediately jumped at the opportunity. I joined the informational meeting to learn more and then committed to going. In August 2011, I flew to Haiti with nineteen other people from our church.

A core tenet of Christianity is to model Jesus in service to others. As I grew in my Christian faith, the desire to serve grew with you. While it is always fulfilling to serve God and the people He calls me to, it can also be difficult, and at times, downright painful.

Nothing could have fully prepared me for what I encountered when we landed in Port-au-Prince, the capital of Haiti. Being that this third-world country was only eight months removed from a devastating earthquake, the airport was in complete shambles and disarray. The terminal's concrete walls were cracked with some parts completely absent. The electricity was unreliable, so many regular airport amenities like directional signs and luggage conveyor belts were not operational.

Due to the lack of sustenance and fear of more earthquakes, Haitians lined up at the airport daily in an attempt to flee the country. They tried to find ways around security in hopes of sneaking onto an outgoing flight. This made lines at the airport nearly impossible to get through. I am sure there was security in the airport, but none was doing much to control the hundreds, if not thousands, of people who were in that airport trying to flee.

Because the conveyor belts weren't operating, our luggage was thrown into a massive pile, which was being picked over by mobs of random people. A few shady characters were trying to steal bags, some pretending to offer help and then taking off with the luggage. We jumped onto and over the conveyor belt into the back area, which would have been off-limits in any US airport, just to grab what we needed. We all stuck together as closely as possible, walking down a narrow fenced-in area to the vehicles that would take us to our destination.

Our team stayed at a large house in Jacmel. The house was surrounded by large block walls and a locked gate that kept outsiders from entering. Crime had risen post-earthquake, and some local criminals targeted missionaries who they believed had items they could steal. Because the government was cycling electricity, the house had power only two hours or so a day. We had no running water due to the fact that most of the city's water was contaminated from the aftereffects of the earthquake. We had to retrieve water daily and filter it to have clean drinking water. We also had no air-conditioning, so the house felt like a steam oven day and night.

The mosquitoes were absolutely disastrous. We were instructed ahead of our trip to pack bug spray. But people don't tell you that applying bug spray is like applying sealant to your skin. It makes your skin and internal body temperature far hotter than it already is from weather conditions. By day two, most of us stopped using bug spray and just dealt with getting bit. It was too hot to have that stuff on.

The worst part of all was trying to sleep, especially that first night. I had never been in conditions like that before, so about halfway through the night as I lay on the bottom bunk in a room with five other guys, I broke into tears and had some sort of anxiety attack. I was freaking out because I could barely breathe, but I was stuck in that third-world country for an entire week. It might sound over-dramatic, but I was losing it. I missed my family and wanted to go home, but I couldn't do that.

Thankfully, God quickly drew me to the people of Haiti to distract me from the difficult conditions. Over the course of the next seven days, our primary goal was to broadly share the love of Jesus while providing practical care, including distribution of toiletries, food, and clothing. We were connected to a couple of local missionaries on the ground, so they took us to various places in the city and spots deep in the jungle.

We set up for a few hours at a time to teach Bible lessons and perform skits to help some better understand Jesus and what He had done for them. We also played an extremely competitive soccer match against some local kids and got smoked, but we had a lot of fun in the process. Nearly every Haitian we met was kind and welcoming. The kids were so sweet that they melted my heart. These experiences eased my anxieties, and I fell in love with people with whom I had no previous connection.

Most will tell you that going on a mission trip, especially a short-term one, is far more impactful on the missionary than it is the people the mission is meant to serve. That is exactly what happened to me. I grew up with a sense of lack when my parents divorced, but I never had to deal with what people of Haiti do. Many lack electricity and running water, walk miles across the jungle to get to their next destination, and are forced to wash their clothes in contaminated streams. Haiti changed me forever, giving me much greater appreciation for all God has blessed me with and also opening my eyes to the need to invest more deeply into God's mission. God calls Christians to preach the gospel to all nations (Matthew 28:18–20).

On the last night of our trip, as some of us hung out on the living room floor, I conversed with my friend and pastor, Tony, who was a leader on the trip. We reflected on the mission and casually chatted about life. "I am so grateful to be here, Tony," I said, "and even more so for your friendship and guidance over the last five years. You and Julee have poured so much into my marriage and my life, and I cannot thank you enough. I know that you will likely be called out to plant a new church soon."

Planting is the act of starting a new church, sometimes birthed from an existing church and other times from scratch, to reach a new group of people in another area. During the five years my family had attended Calvary Chapel East Anaheim, we'd watched a couple of assistant pastors be called out to plant new churches. Michelle and I felt that because of the ways Tony was being used at Calvary to preach and lead others, and the influence he had gained, he would be the next to plant a new church.

"Michelle and I want you to know that we are fully behind you doing that, and want to be there to support you guys in any way we can, whether that be setting up and tearing down for service, doing any menial tasks that we can, or simply sitting in the seats each and every Sunday."

"It's funny that you say that." Tony chuckled, before putting on a serious face. "Julee and I have been talking, and we want you guys to come out and help us plant the church."

"Wait—what?" I had not at all expected that.

"We have been praying about planting another church, as well as what it would look like to do it," Tony shared. "We believe you guys would be a great fit to join us as we do it."

I didn't know all that it would entail, but it was an exciting idea that I was prepared to pursue. More difficult than preparing for the unknown, though, were the challenges of leaving a church and starting a new one, dealing with all the personalities involved, and learning what it means to be a church leader.

THE FIRST WOUND

At the start of 2012, Tony and I officially started the journey to plant a church in Fullerton, California. Along with two other guys, we started meeting to discuss what it would look like to plant a church. What would our church look like and how would it operate? What would be the church's core tenets? What theological principles were most important for us to communicate? How would we lead? Who would serve with us? Who would support us? How would we fund it?

And those were just a few of the hundreds, if not thousands, of questions we had to answer. On top of all that was the fact that none of us had ever planted a church before. And other than Tony, none of the other three of us had been on staff at a church. As we continued to meet and pray, a small group of friends expressed interest in joining our efforts. Over the period of about nine months, our core group was formed.

As all of that was happening, I was fortunate to apply for and get accepted into a pastoral training and biblical studies program that would prepare me to help plant our church. This program was hosted by Mars Hill Church in Seattle, Washington—yes, the Mars Hill led by evangelical pastor Mark Driscoll. It was a huge blessing for two primary reasons. The first was that it was an opportunity for me to gain a formal education of the Bible and biblical leadership. Other than Sundays in church and small group Bible studies, I previously had no deep training or study of the Bible. But Retrain, as it was called, was made up of top present-day pastors, leaders, and teachers. They knew their way around the Bible and church leadership, and that was amazing for me. The second blessing was that it inserted me into a community of like-minded men. Of the 150 people in my class, I estimate that three-quarters of them had either recently planted or were in the process of planting a church. I gained a lot of knowledge from their experiences as they were going through some similar processes. I became very close with a few of those guys, who remain dear friends.

Anyone who has planted a church will tell you how challenging it can be. It comes with struggles to secure space to rent (having your own building is usually out of the question) and to recruit enough volunteers to run the church on Sundays. There's typically not enough money to pay anyone, so everyone still works full-time jobs outside the church, and resources and programs that attract the common churchgoer are often lacking. What made church planting even harder for us was that we did not have support from the church we were leaving. The church leadership was actually opposed to the endeavor and didn't want to lend to our success.

This conflict was the first wound I incurred from the church. On one hand, I understood. It was a large brand-name church, and the leadership of that church wanted to be protective because we weren't carrying on their name. People are protective over things they think are theirs, and in the case of churches, many church leaders believe, or at least act as if, the members of their church are their possession. Therein lies a major issue. Regardless of the sign on the building, church isn't ours—it is Jesus Christ's. He laid down his life, and we are just called to be part of it. Even if we are called to be pastors and leaders, we do so as under-shepherds to Jesus.

But the leadership in our former church wanted to protect its brand, so they all but forced us out of the local area by guilting Tony into believing the godly thing was for us to plant far enough away from them so that we wouldn't be a distraction to their efforts. Tony was kind and obliged, but this suggestion from our former pastor felt like a power grab. Then, some church leaders made unkind and untrue comments about why we were planting a church and even what we believed about the Bible, claiming we were teaching doctrine that was heretical to orthodox Christianity. We chose to maintain our integrity and obliged the church leaders' requests.

While we already had very specific convictions for how we would establish the government and leadership structure in the church, this experience with our former pastor and church further solidified it. To balance power and influence, we committed to starting a church led by a plurality of elders (another Bible term for "pastor"). We knew our rightful place in leadership, as under-shepherds to the true head of the church, Jesus Christ. The flock was His possession, never ours.

Despite the opposition, we officially launched our church plant on September 9, 2012, with three elders, a dozen or so adults, and twenty-plus kids, all meeting inside the lead pastor's house. It was exciting to see nearly a year of prayer come to fruition. While laying a foundation for the next few years was difficult, we formed a small group of members who challenged one another to grow in faith. We celebrated amazing highs, like new jobs, healing of mental and physical ailments, and the birth of babies. We mourned brutal lows including job losses and deaths. Above all, we glorified God collectively and individually, as He called us to.

Church life and leadership for the next eight years was never easy, but God continually showed Himself to be faithful in every aspect of it. That gave me the courage to believe every difficult moment is nothing more than a momentary affliction worth enduring for the sake of that call—until 2020, that is.

THE SECOND WOUND

The year 2020 was challenging for every person on this planet, due to the COVID-19 pandemic. Adding to that challenge in America was racial tension that led to civil unrest, riots, and a dividing line in our country. Those two major issues came with significant challenges for every church leader, but for me, they eventually led to my leaving the church I helped plant.

It may surprise you to hear that of all the wounds I cite in this book, this one is the most difficult to share. The Christian church, particularly in America, has been the target of so much unwarranted hate and accusation. People in some of those churches, claiming to be Christians, have committed horrific sins and even committed awful crimes. The church has been stained by some of the men and women in it, and I don't want to add to it. But it would be inauthentic of me to exclude this wound from my book, because it's part of my story—and part of the way God has led me to be the man he calls me to be.

I want to be clear in stating that I do not believe anybody is perfect, including myself. I am certain there were times I could have been more gracious, generous, or understanding, and I am very sorry to anyone I hurt. Also, I do not believe any of the situations I share on the following pages was meant to intentionally hurt me. I believe we have all been created with unique passions and perspectives, and sometimes standing firm in strong beliefs ends up hurting others. The actions taken by those around me were very likely carried out in ways they believed would best serve the people they were leading and loving.

To set the scene, the pandemic and racial tension in America caused congregations across the nation to butt heads and even fracture over conflicts about personal and political beliefs. Church leaders did their best just to maintain the church and its well-being. When it came to the pandemic, we asked questions like these: "Do we stop meeting in person?" "When do we meet in person again?" "Do we require masks?" "Do we follow everything state and local governments mandate?"

We read science journals and news reports to learn what we could, reached out to other church leaders to gain perspective on what they were doing, and did our best to abide by the laws and guidance of the government without being disobedient to the word of God. When we planted the church nearly eight years prior, nobody prepared us for such extreme social shifts.

As it related to the racial tension, we asked questions such as these: "How do we address this?" "When do we speak up, and when do we stay silent?" "How do we support church members struggling through specific issues, including those being mistreated because of their race as well as others trying to eradicate racial bias in their hearts?"

We paid attention to current events and listened to many wise people throughout the season. We studied God's word, to inform everything we said and did as it pertained to the issue of racial tension. While it is absolutely clear that God does not support any form of racism, navigating people's perspectives on what falls into that category became quite difficult. Tensions rose in our church's group messaging chats, during small group discussions, and even at large meetings of church members.

Much of the church community in America divided over these issues in very unhealthy ways. Unfortunately for our small church plant, similar division occurred. I do not believe anyone was intentionally trying to divide our church, but some members' actions were not gracious or godly. Opinions took precedent over God's word. One such instance was when an article, titled "40 Ways for White People to Not Be Racist," was shared in our group messaging chat, which the entire church body participated in.

Further, more sermons were preached on the "topics of the day," including racism and bias. While it is always important to speak to social issues, I feel the pulpit is not the place to primarily focus on current events. The main event on the pulpit has been, is, and will always be to preach the *good news*: Jesus Christ lived a perfect life, died a sinner's death, and defeated sin and death by rising from the grave so every person who puts their faith in Him will be reconciled to God and given eternal life with Him.

The Bible definitely speaks to race, gender, sexuality, and politics, so we cannot ignore these issues. But the best way to address all those issues, and questions that arise from them, is by preaching the good news of Christ. To make the main point of a sermon something other than Jesus is to completely miss the mark. Granted, every pastor likely makes the mistake of overemphasizing a topic they really care about, but that doesn't make it right. Separate forums, outside the Sunday sermon, are better suited for detailed discussion of specific topics. We hosted a few such forums, but for some members in our church, those weren't enough.

Many people in our church were hurting. They were shut in and closed off from friends and family, due to pandemic restrictions. They were also watching the people of our country divide and, in many cases, attempt to destroy one another, while experiencing division inside their own church. I wanted to help them, as did the other two pastors in the church. I spoke up when I saw issues directly affecting church members and, more often than not, felt my opinions were quickly shut down or discounted.

I am the first to admit I am pretty firm in my convictions, and I had strong opinions about how we should handle the pandemic and address the racial tensions. With the pandemic, I was fully on board with being overly cautious and conservative to protect from unknown health risks. But as some data rolled in, allowing certain businesses and public settings, but not the church, to welcome people back in, I became pretty adamant about defying the government order and meeting together in person. While the church should do its best to obey the laws of the land, I feel we are called to obey God first. God commands His people to regularly gather at the local church, with wisdom and safety in mind. My recommendation was quickly shut down, even among our leadership team.

I also introduced a different perspective as to some of the issues around race. For example, I pointed out the fact that race is not the motivation behind all arrests of Black men by police officers who are not Black. I also maintained that, the property damage and violence committed during the 2020 riots were wrong, despite the wrongs that motivated the riotous acts. I was often shot down or looked down upon, in part perhaps because I am white, which seemed to diminish my credibility in conversations around race. I understand full well that I will never know what it is like to live as a person of color, but that doesn't mean my thoughts, opinions, and feelings are unimportant.

The Bible says we are all members of one body, though different, and that the entire body needs every member (1 Corinthians 12:12–27). All voices—and hearts—matter, especially in dealing with charged topics. God gives me His Spirit of love and care for all people, and I am confident I can use that to benefit any topic of conversation, even one on race.

Many others in our congregation, including whites and people of color, had opinions similar to mine on issues related to the pandemic and race. They brought their concerns to me because they knew we were aligned and also felt uncomfortable sharing them with the other leaders. I then shared their concerns in our leadership discussions, feeling called as their church elder to speak on their behalf. But wasn't heard fairly in those situations either. As time went on, I felt exhausted and beat down.

This battle finally came to a head in July 2020. I was frustrated by the words and actions of people that I was seeing in public discourse, and I shared my opinion about it on Twitter. Within minutes, I received a rude and condescending message from a pastor's wife, accusing me of using my position of influence, both publicly and in our local church community, to quiet the voices of marginalized groups, particularly women and people of color. *How dare she say that!* I thought. I was in complete disbelief. I handed my phone to my wife, Michelle, so she could read the message and confirm I wasn't crazy or overreacting.

For context, my wife is Hispanic and I am white, so my two children are of mixed ethnicity. I work very hard to build them up, lift them, and help them achieve practical equality in this world. The primary way I do that is by showing them what God says about them. I want my children to know, as stated in Genesis 1:27, that they are made in God's image. And Psalm 139:14 promises they are fearfully and wonderfully made. Those two verses alone are proof positive that the God of this universe created them with an eternal imprint, assigning a level of value and worth found only in Christ.

Ironically, I spent much of that season encouraging my kids that it was OK to be white. My oldest daughter, then seventeen, often overemphasized her Latin heritage in conversations with classmates because some looked down on her for her pale skin. I helped her see that God created all of her, that he was proud of who He made her to be, and that her white skin made her no less of a person than anyone else.

What hurt so much about the interaction with that pastor's wife was that I had spent more than eight years supporting, encouraging, and elevating her inside and outside of our church. In a single instant, the trust and respect she and I had spent so many years building was broken.

I sent an email to the other two pastors, letting them know I needed a sabbatical. I explained that I was exhausted and needed a break. After nearly eight years of pastoring, I was long overdue for some extended time off. But what really frustrated me was my fellow pastor, my friend, knew his wife had confronted me, and he was completely silent. They'd both been beside me on my entire journey of restoration and transformation—my marriage, my relationship with my dad, my career challenges, the aftermath of the Route 91 tragedy, and so much more. Up until that moment, I felt as if they were grafted into my life forever—and on the other side of heaven, that is true. But we were no longer close friends on this side of heaven.

UNEXPECTED TRANSITION

My intention for the sabbatical was to take three months off beginning in August 2020 and then come back just after Thanksgiving weekend. I felt I could rest and recharge, seek counsel for what had gone on in the church, and receive guidance on how best to reenter my role. But being on sabbatical didn't mean my family would take a break from church. We needed to continue being fed God's word and worshiping with God's people.

Through a good friend, I knew of a solid church, Southlands Church, near my house. We decided to check it out. From the first Sunday we joined under a makeshift tent in the front parking lot, we loved everything about the church. It had solid Bible teaching, great worship, and kind people.

A few weeks into visiting, I introduced myself to the lead pastor, Alan Frow. From the moment I met him, I could tell that Alan was a true shepherd leader. His body language and cool South African accent drew me into his presence with a great sense of godly welcome and comfort. I shared that I was a pastor on sabbatical with my family. He invited me to chat more, so we set up a coffee meeting for the next week.

At that meeting, I openly shared my struggles over the years with church planting, issues in the church, and how I felt hurt. Being that Alan had been a pastor for nearly two decades and came from South Africa, where much greater problems had existed, I knew he would share wisdom as it related to where I needed to grow, what I needed to let go, and what could change at my church for me to serve there in a healthy manner. I respected the fact that in that meeting, and in the future, Alan did not ever tell me what to do. He pointed to scripture and offered guidance on what to consider in all the issues I was facing.

During one particular church service, I had an overwhelming feeling of peace and clarity. It wasn't the sermon specifically, or even a song, but the cumulative experiences my family and I had enjoyed while attending. Sitting in our lawn chairs on an asphalt parking lot due to pandemic restrictions, I felt completely comfortable and at home. *Maybe my time as a pastor has come to an end*, I thought. I couldn't believe I was thinking that. I loved being a pastor. I loved preaching God's word, and I loved leading, guiding, and supporting others through my church role. But I felt I could no longer, with a joyful heart and in good conscience, serve at my church in that capacity.

When I shared that feeling with my Michelle, she was instantly on board. Understand that she never makes quick or rash decisions. She is always slow to decide and thinks through her options. But she had felt the same as I was feeling and for far longer. She'd felt hurt by people at our church, and she'd seen my kids hurt by people at our church. To be clear, these were emotional hurts from broken relationships or the alienation of not fitting in. My wife and kids were supportive of me in my pastoral role for all those years and never once asked me to step down. But when I brought up the idea, they were all ready to go. That was all the affirmation I needed. I wanted to meet with the other two pastors one final time to share my thoughts.

My meeting with the other two pastors provided even more confirmation. I brought up a few lingering issues, but my words were immediately discounted as unwarranted. I couldn't believe they didn't see these issues as problematic, or perhaps they didn't want to see them. Either way, I took it as the final sign that my time leading at that church had come to an end. My family and I attended one final church service there so we could say goodbye to all of the people we co-labored with for so many years. A few, including the other two pastors, got up after the service to say some kind words about me and my family. They were heartfelt, and I appreciated that.

I am grateful for the time we spent together. I hold lots of grace for the imperfect ways we navigated church leadership. While I have put our issues in the past, I was not able to fully heal from them for a few years. The conflicts in that church festered, and approximately one year after I left, the church shut down. That broke my heart. The wounds I incurred calloused my heart to church leadership.

Just as every other wound in my life was ultimately a way for God to strengthen me, the Wound of Church opened me up to a new spiritual path He was calling me to. Stepping down from my pastoring role was extremely difficult, but it led us to our permanent church—Southlands in Brea, California.

I have been restored by Alan and other pastors of the church. I am involved in a weekly men's Bible study, which constantly helps me grow as a husband and father. My wife and I attend a weekly community group in which we have developed deep friendships with amazing people. My youngest daughter is in love with her youth group and is building wonderful friendships. My oldest daughter's boyfriend was baptized in the church on Easter Sunday 2022. They attend church with us every Sunday. Our family feels like we are at home.

APPLYING THE WOUND-ANALYSIS FRAMEWORK

Acknowledge the hurt.

The wound of church was the result of being mentally and emotionally hurt by leaders and members in the first church my family attended as well as the church I helped plant and pastor.

Realize the effect.

The wound of church affected my life in three major ways:

1. My family came to faith at that first church and served there for many years. We loved its people and leaders. That made feeling misrepresented when we planted our own church so much more hurtful. I expect people to rejoice when God's

word spreads and His family grows, but unfortunately that is not always the case.

2. Being called to pastor a church is a huge blessing. At the same time, it can be very challenging. I am grateful for the ways I grew into that role, but I am also sorry for, early in my ministry, hurting people by being overzealous or immature.

3. The biggest hurt of all came during my final season of church leadership. To be discounted, and even cast out, because I had a different opinion was cutting. We had been through so much together over the years, so to watch it all fade away was heartbreaking.

Unlock the greatness.

God used the wound of church to strengthen my faith in Him.

That difficult season caused me to pray more and seek more of God. Seeing church leaders' missteps, and acknowledging my own, strengthened my knowing that God is the only perfect leader. He can always be depended on. His word is the only truth, ever reliable. His Spirit never fails to lead me to the precise places I need to go.

Seeing God in greater ways firms up my faith that more greatness is still ahead for me. Greatness awaits you, too. True greatness requires you to stop running from or ignoring your wounds. Recognize that God is prepared to use your wounds to show you how great He is—and how much greatness he has lined up for you.

Conclusion

I WOULD DO JUST ABOUT ANYTHING TO HAVE AVOIDED ALL OF THE wounds I've shared with you.

I wish I could have stopped the Route 91 gunman before he started shooting, saving the lives of fifty-eight people, including Nicol, while protecting the other twenty-two thousand from a life of fear, anxiety, and mental, emotional, and physical scars. I wish I could exist in large crowds of people without thinking about the nearest exit or a suspicious-looking person across the room.

I wish I could take back every hurtful word I ever said to Michelle and every action that made her feel unappreciated or unloved. I wish I could say I've always honored her in our marriage.

And, I wish my dad had never left. That was the beginning of a decades-long storm that distorted my views of myself and the world around me.

But each wound was meant to happen. Reflecting back, I can say confidently that they bettered me. These wounds revealed areas of my life and character that needed to improve or change, peeled back layers necessary to reveal my true calling and giving me confidence to be all God created me to be.

By God's grace and the wisdom He's given me, I have turned each wound into the following key strengths, both personal and professional.

STRENGTHS FOR PERSONAL GREATNESS

I learned how to be a better husband after almost losing my marriage, a near end that came as the result of my acting like an absolute idiot at times—disrespecting my wife, not valuing her, and putting my needs over hers. Our marriage is flourishing after more than twenty-two years, and I believe that might not have been possible without nearly losing it. I needed to see my wife's value as a woman and as my partner. I needed to make her my number one priority in life. As a husband, I am called to lead, provide for, and protect Michelle, and for the rest of my life I will do that to the best of my ability.

Claiming victory over a near-failed marriage, I have taken up the mission of helping other men and women succeed in their marriages. It can be far too easy to make marriage about expecting your spouse to fulfill your every need. That's not only wrong—it's impossible. I am using the platform God has given me to encourage husbands to be leaders, providers, and protectors. I help couples establish fair and reasonable expectations, healthy boundaries, and honest and respectful communication. I inspire couples to forgive and ask for forgiveness, to unconditionally love each other, and to put God at the center of their marriage.

I am now a better father to my children. While I always loved my kids, I regularly served my own needs by working longer hours to fulfill my desires. By poorly treating my wife, their mom, I was giving them a bad example of what a husband should be and what a wife should expect, accept, or tolerate in marriage. I love my daughters with all of my heart and spend as much time with them as I possibly can. I have a responsibility to set a standard for the type of person they will marry and to model great expectations for what a healthy, godly marriage looks like.

I also learned how to be a better son. I had a lot of maturing to do and too often expected my dad to be perfect. I should have much sooner accepted his requests to reconnect. I could have lost the opportunity to reunite with my dad had something tragic happened to him during the time we were apart. We now have an incredible relationship and enjoy much time together on the phone and in person. I see how much he loves me, and that makes me love him so much more.

I learned how to be a better human being in this world. I'd say most of my life I have been a "good guy." But being a good guy came up short, causing me to hurt other people and damage my own life. I have to see people as God sees them—men and women created in His image and, therefore, of eternal worth and value. Nobody is more or less important than another. I see people differently, embracing them as humans with unique wounds, and in need of someone to listen and care. I desire to make every conversation and every encounter matter. I try to make time for anyone who needs me, pouring out every bit of wisdom God wills me to share in order to help them be their best.

STRENGTHS FOR PROFESSIONAL GREATNESS

When I began coaching in 2011, I had a talent for sales and a passion to help others succeed. Early on, those were great drivers for me. But I learned that talent and passion are not sufficient in achieving greatness.

I, like many, tried to rely on natural skill and natural will. Natural skill and natural will got me pretty far along on my professional journey, but they also created a lot of serious issues. My biggest issues were selfishness and self-reliance. I'd built my whole life around myself, in turn setting myself up for complete failure. When I failed, I tried to do even more by myself.

Instead of being humble enough to ask for help when my business was struggling, I pridefully pretended I had it together. I took more of the same approaches that weren't working, further creating burdens I could not bear. Heavily burdened mentally and emotionally, I couldn't possibly show up as my best self for my clients, so my ability to exhibit peak professional performance was significantly hindered. Nobody—even those of us who think we can be superheroes—can succeed alone.

God broke me, showing me that alone I am incapable of true greatness. He showed me that, first and foremost, I need His strength, sustenance, guidance, and wisdom. He also showed me that, to be my best self, I need other people—their love and care, experiences and expertise, emotional and practical support. I was good on my own. But with God and the people He surrounds me with, I can be great.

God used my wounds to reshape me. He strengthened me with new abilities to look outside myself, see inside other people, recognize their inner greatness, and bring that greatness to the surface to help them be and achieve all God has planned for them. "Grateful" cannot even begin to describe how I feel about God working through me in this way. While it feels amazing to build a business I love and that supports my family, it feels even better to know God blesses me with the ability to impact the lives of those I am so fortunate to work with.

Executives, entrepreneurs, and sales professionals most often hire me as a performance coach to help them achieve financial goals typically related to income and revenue. I help them develop the systems, processes, mindsets, and habits to achieve those goals. I stand with them in encouragement and accountability to ensure they take necessary steps to achieve their desired goals.

But the real growth and goal achievement happens when we go deeper, when I utilize the Wound-Analysis Framework to help clients uncover fear, doubt, regret, or shame smoldering inside of them. Acknowledging the cause and impact of those underlying emotions helps them use their wounds to achieve the greatness for which God created them. This greatness includes the financial goals clients initially hired me to help them achieve. All of my clients rave about the fact that when I coach them, they not only become better professionally but also personally. They feel more in control of and

CONCLUSION

fulfilled in their personal daily lives. Support in producing those outcomes brings my greatest fulfillment as a coach!

The anxiety attack I suffered in 2019 wouldn't be my last, nor was it the last time I would be wounded. By applying the Wound-Analysis Framework to new wounds, I am better equipped to minimize their impact on me and to move forward more quickly and with stronger emotional reserves.

I didn't write this book just to tell my story. I wrote it to demonstrate that God created *you* for greatness. Your life story, even when it hurts or gets messy, is a testimony to the lengths God goes to show you how great you can be. I hope and pray you'll use the Wound-Analysis Framework to heal wounds you currently bear as well as those that are still to come…because they will come. Acknowledge the hurt inflicted on you, realize its effect on your life, and unlock God's greatness in you!

Acknowledgments

I WOULDN'T BE WHERE I AM WITHOUT THE LOVE AND SUPPORT of the following people.

To my amazing wife and best friend, Michelle. You have cheered louder for me than anyone, been the first to call me out on my b.s., loved me in ways I don't deserve, and show me every single day how to live the life Jesus calls me to. I wouldn't be the man I am without you.

To my beautiful daughters, Alexis and Chloe. You are amazing gifts and I am honored that God called me to be your dad.

To my mom, Carol. You fought against all odds and gave up so much of your own life to give me mine.

To my dad, James. You blessed me with so much wisdom and drive and instilled values into me that have led to the success I have been blessed to achieve

To my stepmom, Madeline. You accepted me as your own from the moment we met and have always made me feel so loved and cared for.

To my stepdad, Tom. You showed me what honor and integrity really were and helped me to adopt those qualities as my own.

To my brother Cory. You have over and over again showed me what perseverance looks like and I thank God that we are thriving today because of that.

To my fellow survivors, Chad, Casey, Heather, Tracy. We share a bond that will never be broken and you have a piece of my heart that will never be taken away.

To our fallen angel, Nicol. The world was robbed of your infectious smile and beautiful soul, but your legacy will live on in our hearts forever.

To my Framily. You are the best friends and craziest family members a guy could ask for and I love you all so much.

And to everyone else who has supported and encouraged me, thank you!

Most importantly, to my Lord and Savior Jesus Christ. You chased me down and rescued me, you showed me who you created me to be, and you've given me more than I deserve.

Made in the USA
Middletown, DE
01 September 2024

60175812R00099